# SIDESHOW CONCESSIONS

# SIDESHOW CONCESSIONS

Lucas Crawford

**SNARE**

Invisible Publishing
Halifax & Toronto

Library and Archives Canada Cataloguing in Publication

Crawford, Lucas, 1983-, author
    Sideshow concessions / Lucas Crawford.

(Robert Kroetsch Award for Innovative Poetry)
Poems.
Issued in print and electronic formats.
ISBN 978-1-926743-57-8 (paperback).--ISBN 978-1-926743-63-9 (epub)

    I. Title.

PS8605.R43S54 2015          C811'.6          C2015-905244-0
                                             C2015-905245-9

Edited by Leigh Nash

Cover and interior design by Megan Fildes | Typeset in Laurentian and Slate
With thanks to type designer Rod McDonald

Printed and bound in Canada

Invisible Publishing | Halifax & Toronto
www.invisiblepublishing.com

We acknowledge the support of the Canada Council for the Arts which last year invested $20.1 million in writing and publishing throughout Canada.

Invisible Publishing recognizes the support of the Province of Nova Scotia through the Department of Communities, Culture & Heritage. We are pleased to work in partnership with the Culture Division to develop and promote our cultural resources for all Nova Scotians.

I.
## Fattest Man In The World

Your Fat Daughter Remembers What You Said                          1

How Families Mourn When They Have Money
And Don't Know Each Other                                          7

Memorandum For The Fellows At The Gym                             10

Recurring Questions From The Summer
I Didn't Leave The House                                          14

Stop All The Clocks On Pancake Tuesday                           16

Eating Chinese In Kingston, Nova Scotia (Population: 5174)       26

My Fattest Aunt                                                   29

Please Don't Bury Me Down In That Cold, Cold Ground              31

One Of My Thin Friends                                            34

Chairs And Stages Can't Contain Me                                36

My Last Meal                                                      38

Failed Seances For Rita Macneil (1944–2013)                      40

II.
## Bearded Lady

Long Twisted Things                                               48

Introducing The Letter Ex (1)                                     49

Scar Tissue Looks Good On Pomquet Beach                           50

Airplane Lavatory Algebra                                         52

Introducing The Letter Ex (2)     55

O, Adulthood     56

The Force Required To Occupy My
Shirt Is Stronger Than Gravity     57

Introducing The Letter Ex (3)     59

Monogamy (A Lost Letter For Reading Aloud)     60

III.
**Sword Swallower**

Road Rules     64

Canadian Literature Premises     66

Introducing The Letter Ex (4)     72

I Got An A+ On The Test Because
I Couldn't Stop Rereading     74

Infomercials     75

Muzzled     77

Depression     79

Letters, In Any Case     81

Introducing The Letter Ex (5)     83

The Hand Unlearns To Touch     84

Cruising Utopia     86

Dear Mrs. Luberto     89

# I.
# FATTEST MAN IN THE WORLD

# YOUR FAT DAUGHTER REMEMBERS WHAT YOU SAID

My dad was in the hospital cafeteria
eating lasagna when I was born.
I was making lasagna at home when he flat-lined.

>                              Symmetry.

My mom has low blood pressure. My dad's was high. And I
am a gymnastics school dropout
with an inherited need to redefine balance.
(I sat immovable on the seesaw,
a whole pubescent pack
trying to dethrone me.)

I'm fifteen, telling my parents I'm gay. Dad says:

> *I know you think you are*
> *'cause you're a bigger girl*
> *and boys don't like you.*

>                   I start a list of his remarks like this.

When his heart stopped for the first time,
I was making lasagna with my first girlfriend.
She was closeted and was supposed to be elsewhere,
maybe on an elephant eating cardamom marshmallows and
counting every lucky constellation that she and her father
can't find in the light-drowned night sky of Mumbai.

*There you were when you were skinny as a rail!*
*Dad says this when we all watch an old video.*
I am four in the video.
*Lighten up, he's just trying to encourage you!*

Encourage me to *what*?

Choose a photograph from your hard drive.
Invert the colours.
Stare at it for thirty seconds. Close your eyes,
then open them in front of a flat white wall.
Now, each time you blink, you will see the photograph
as if it's been branded on your insides.
I'm sure that somewhere a nun is doing this
with a digitized painting of white hippie Jesus.
She's shrieking with vengeful glee,
"*That* is the power of the holy spirit!"
The image is everywhere and nowhere, but it's no spirit.
It is a matter of light and the physics of memory.
It is the way in which bad memories might reappear
each night and blink.

Even if trauma is so last season.

*You are going to trim your chin hairs*
*for your grandmother's funeral.*
*Oh yes, you can see them.*
*I was noticing them in the light the other day*
*and it would mean a lot to us.*
*Get your sister to help you do it.*
*Girls don't have chin hair.*

My dad had coarse curls, salt-and-pepper 'stache,
and a neck beard.
My mother's family has coifs that go Brillo Pad in Atlantic air.
I have it all, from chin to chubby toes.
How was I to know
that I ought to be ashamed
to be the heir apparent
to my parents' hair?

*You thought holy communion was a snack?*
*You would think that.*

Months before he died,
my dad carried a small portable cabin
through the woods with a buddy and said,
            *If that doesn't kill me, nothing will.*
Irony is the new black, Dad,
and you know it's slimming.

*You'll be 200 pounds*
*by the time you're in Grade Eight.*
(CHALLENGE ACCEPTED.)

I was eating smoked meat yesterday on the boulevard
and noticed that the goods are measured on a silver scale
emblazoned with the slogan: "We Weigh the World."
The same company produces a tool called a "strain gauge,"
which indicates how much pressure
is being put upon an object.
I saw a picture of a strain gauge
glued across a crack in a brick house.

Am I the house or the gauge
or am I the picketer with a placard that says
            "The possibility of collapse
            cannot be determined by formula—"

            *I'm sorry I've been so hard on ya.*
            *Don't want you to end up like me.*

*Lose weight* was the last thing my dad ever said to me
but I don't think it was the first.

The sea that crashes in my stomach is percussive:
dozens of Captain Morgan mickeys
clink as they bob atop the waves;
voices recite the messages stuffed in those bottles;
heavy ambient ocean air drowns them out.

His last words echoed
with the empty-theatre hollowness of his own gut,
with the hum of capsizing winds passing over the beer
bottles that sat in his stomach.
They were jammed with
his mother's own abusive misspellings
and with fortunes that didn't come true.

> *Is it possible to hate a ghost*
> *who has always already*
> *haunted himself*
> *through you?*

I'm doing just fine.

I rub my stomach when it gets choppy.

I still check my vital signs when I microwave lasagna.

I eat lots of berries.

I dip my mozzarella sticks in ranch.

I've known since age four how to tell a lightning rod
from a switch from an olive branch.

I have these dreams where I'm floating.
Where I wave down to my chiropractor,
my old music teacher, and my dad.
All I know is that I'm going really far away
and when I wake up, I can't remember if
the dreaming-I was sad.

# HOW FAMILIES MOURN WHEN THEY HAVE MONEY AND DON'T KNOW EACH OTHER

I.
You ransacked his rumpus room
and sold his collection of kaleidoscopes.
The family got along while you tripped over bonds
and stocks in his stowaway cellar.
You wore a periwinkle skirt
and weed-green shirt for the funeral.
*I didn't want anyone to think*
*that I had dressed for convention's sake.*

II.
As a young seaman, your father watched a ship explode.
Men became lava, then steam, and settled as ash on water.
He never talked about it.
Maybe it's all he could see with his naked eyes.

III.
There's no home for atheists in that town,
so you stood at a church lectern to blazon him.
You were so angry about it that you kicked the side of a car,
the owner of which was hidden in the back of the annex,
counting that week's collection plate
with a coinage tool made for casinos and couch-surfers.
I have never been surprised enough
to manage indignation when my will isn't done.

IV.
He made you repeat the mental map you'd need
to find the rare coins buried out back.
Now you step slowly, shovel on shoulder
and feel like a sad new-age pirate.
You all lent a hand digging up the backyard's
brick path laid with gold Krugerrands.
You wore red shoes to the funeral
and received many compliments.

V.
Every Halloween, he handed out the state's best loot bags.
(The local paper covered it.)
His was oil money and I wonder if he was slick.
You asked him to stop giving you
so many Christmas presents, but he refused.
As Beckett said: "Against the charitable gesture there is no
defence, that I know of."

VI.
The night of the funeral, you lit the sky
with his fireworks collection.
You took a photo of the powdered ash on snow
that was left after the show.
Everyone would know that this family
was not sitting sad at home.
Neighbours will remark:
*they are puncturing the sky*
*with colour and smoke. They are happy.*
Your mom bought a condo and enrolled in adult-ed classes.

VII.
You tell me that your mother doesn't know
you at all and that he didn't either.
You didn't cry. Your right eye stopped
working for a few days from your MS.
Your brain fills in the "blind spot" with images
you've stared at over the past decade—
a book cover, an intricate key, a milk-carton lost child,
except they look like woodcuts.
You say you are doing just fine.
Your mother gave you ten thousand dollars.
You can only look at me squinting, awry.
You say you are doing just fine.

## MEMORANDUM FOR
## THE FELLOWS AT THE GYM

I see your biceps, triceps, and quadriceps,
except I'm not interested!
>    250 pounds of man muscle?
>    A flexed neck?
>    Erect pecs?
Next to you
a stone looks soft.
(And kind of smart.)
>    Take heart—I joke, I poke.
>    Don't be so neurotic;
>    I *like* guys (and no, not even
>    just platonically).

With your
taut tights,
torn tops,
cutoffs,
dance music,
mirrored walls and
those stretched shorts
that reveal your upper thighs,
I only wish you military men knew
how closely your gym resembles my gay bar.
Although martini-free,
I see you drinking that *pink* Gatorade.
>    Replenishing your electrolytes, my ass.

Crass poetry falls on iPodded ears that fear...what?
Human interaction?    Distraction
                      from your ParticipACTION?
                      Hal Johnson and Joanne McLeod
                      would be proud, but how'd you like
                      to sculpt a way for us to coexist here?

My pounds were lost,
but now they're found:
dissertation pounds,
falling out of love pounds,
in the doghouse pounds,
studying TS Eliot and Ezra Pound pounds.
Pouncing on my roundness with dumbbells,
as if I want to be square like you.

          You: shoulders steeled, serious.
          Me? I could show you how to be delirious.
          I could be your "roll" model
          because I know the bliss of being malleable,
          of becoming a text that tells of flesh bending.
                      I *want* to let my limbs surprise, guys.

Public nudity is not an adventure
for those who need to feel secure.
I'm the fattest chap in the world, but sure,
I'll get naked in the vacant ladies' locker room,
assuming (foolishly) that one-hundred staring hotties
won't shuffle in with duffle bags, muffling laughs
at this worn, unadorned, shorn-haired dyke.

But boys, it's you who have gall,
standing tall, your legs sprawled,
constantly rearranging your balls.
But you look so mad
when I dare to
adjust my
bloody
manly
maxi-
pad.
It's
some
messed-up
mathematics
        that makes sweating blood studly
        but requires secreting it be a secret.
        Only strengths need to be silenced
        to the degree of crinkle-free pad wrappers
        or tampons smaller than a piece of gum.

Chew on that!

Fit: adjective meaning suitable, adequate, appropriate.
When did becoming thoroughly average
start to seem like such a good goal?
Next time you're powerlifting,
that's something new you'll need to work out.

Because I see your biceps, triceps, quadriceps,
except what interests me, I'll divulge,
are *not* muscles that bulge.

# RECURRING QUESTIONS FROM THE
# SUMMER I DIDN'T LEAVE THE HOUSE

I. When Dad was
   conscious for that
   stop-watched
   second, did he wink
   *only* at me?

II. Urns are one-
    size fits-all. Does
    anyone deserve
    to go home half
    in a baggie?

III. Is there money
     to be made
     in the eulogy-
     ghostwriting business?

IV. When I farted
    during a play
    in Grade Eight, did anyone
    know it was
    me? Did
    *every*one?

V. On a rare visit from
high school
"friends," one of
them pointed out
that I'd worn the
same brown T-shirt
every time she saw
me that summer.
Why did she say it?

VI. Was Gilmora Hall
really haunted by
"the blue nun,"
a jilted priest-
lover who leapt
to her death
in the courtyard
and chased down
nighttime
bathroom
users?

VII. Did I just hear
a noise?

# STOP ALL THE CLOCKS ON
# PANCAKE TUESDAY

For Lent, I will give up sleeping with my professor.

In class, I superimpose her family stories over her lectures:
a mother who served them breast milk soufflé;
a father who hocked Amway;
a brother middle-named Lampshade just for fun;
and, the mysterious family car
that changed colours in the sun.

For Lent, I will write up one memory of her per day
in red ink, on the back of my term papers
until every page looks like a stoplight.
I'll tape them up backwards on my all-girls dorm-room wall
where nuns hung crosses until last year.
Let the tape strip off stripes of paint when I move home.
Let the resultant mosaic of quick-rip scars
remind the next resident about the benefits
of slow, steady detachment.

> **DAY ONE**
> The day I brought her a bag of red licorice.
> She said nobody had done anything so thoughtful
> for her for as long as she could recall.
> She cried, and, except for when Dad had died
> the year before,
> I'd never felt so sad.

For Lent, I will bundle up my thoughts
of this smiling antagonist town
with its thousand hidden sins
and bury them in the causeway
that links us to an island.
Let the waves lap up over my boring shame
and smooth them down to stone.
Let me drive through this island one day
and find that queer Catholic guilt repurposed as folk art
for sale from a road-shoulder shanty.
In ten years, let this folk art
with its cracked green and yellow paint
sit on the floor holding a heavy wooden door open
for some student out west whose mother
tucked the rock inside her carry-on.

For Lent, I will give thanks for paradoxical university towns
where frowns are for home and the Chinese restaurant
is resplendent in tartan decor. Nobody believes
the rumour they hear about you because
if it were true, surely they'd have heard before now.
*Jesus b'y, no way she's got a girl on the side!*
*She's married to some other prof!*

**DAY TWO**
When she told me that after storage-sifting,
she'd found her favourite sweater
and realized it was older than me.
Was its vague hue (swamp + rainbow +
white noise) an omen?

**DAY THREE**
Her bemused disappointment
when I sliced her fancy party cheeses
into piles and piles of cubes
to look like a grocery store deli tray.
The cubes looked like crumbling bricks,
the tray a diorama of Parmesan ruins.

For Lent, I will become seven again.
Pledges of abstinence were more fun then
when we'd chatter about who had given up
chocolate and who sacrificed potato chips.
Lent is a popular time for grade schoolers
to begin doubting the power of categories:
*Cinnamon hearts aren't really a candy, are they?*
*Aren't they more of a spice? Hey, did you know*
*that black liquorice comes from a plant?*

For Lent, I will punish myself
by *not* telling my mother what's happened.
Every time we talk, I will hunch over—
a micro-mortification of the flesh
that will never be known to those
unwilling to risk an unironic moment.
I perspire with the panic of the Confessional stammer.
Let this sweat evaporate, become rain,
and someday rise as steam
from a humidifier that will let a girl clear her throat and speak.

### DAY FOUR
How she walked home through traffic
from the hospital on the hill
after doing no-breakfast blood work at 7 AM.
How angry her husband was
that I requested she take an HIV test.
She is twice my age; he is twice hers.
He lived without contagions or computers,
    I without vinyl or busy signals.

**DAY FIVE**
Her very first come-on, at her book launch
sliding her hand onto my sacrum, inside
the back of my jeans, just above my
overworked old underwear. I couldn't imagine
that soon she would slice me up.
That she would steep my feet with beets,
my ears with pears, my kidneys with beans—offal.
My minor organs jarred, cellared, sold by her
at the farmer's market without so much as a
shooter of local anesthetic or a goodbye.

For Lent, I will rub Wednesday ashes on myself
as a way to externalize sentiment.
I'll smear it not only into the fault lines of my forehead
but also into the grimy folds of the elbows in which I held her.
Let this ash derive from old wood,
perhaps from the kitchen table
she sanded and refinished before moving to Nova Scotia.
Her favourite students lined this table nearly nightly
breaking bread and booze. One day when she was gone
to fetch the next case of red wine, her other disciples and I
flipped the table and signed it with a black magic marker.
Let this table come from a tree in BC,
from land that changed hands like a bomb drops.
If this tree once shaded someone

who knew how, properly,
to be an elder
then amen.
I am only religious about
epic reckonings
and metaphors.

### DAY SIX
Her story about the week they moved here
about how three guys had been hitting golf balls
at the field where they do the Highland Games.
She and her husband happened
upon the trio hooting
about how they'd "hit Buddy's car over d'ere!"
She didn't realize that "Buddy"
is both a vague anybody
and also a specific island fiddler
who needs a last name
around here no more than Madonna or Jesus.

### DAY SEVEN
The summer when she gained some weight
and said her thighs rubbed together so much
that she was excited all the time.
The week she told me this, she burned down
an old stump in their backyard.
It was a season of many burning bushes.

For Lent, I will ignore the students
she and her husband currently favour.
I will hand out lukewarm smiles like Halloween candy and
impersonate those who are experts in moderation and silence.
As with a stale candy kiss, I will chew to no avail and only
feel the anger grow larger in my chops.
I'll swallow it one day like tight old gum,
but I know it's I who has stuck in her gut
for eight years or more.

### DAY EIGHT
Her long-infused vodka-lime breath
that might've ignited with just sun.
She huffed through tears
that she was sorry to love me.
She had chased me home
to my dorm at sunrise.

**DAY NINE**
Weeks later, going to her class late
after having two pineapple coolers
at Piper's Pub on my way back
from my mother's great-aunt's wake.
Laughing at the scolding email she sent later
because everything she writes smells
of someone who has never lost. No—
of someone who stings with
     the sad grasp
     of her own
     normalcy.

**DAY TEN**
Is the day when Lent does us in.
Is hurried potato chips in the bathroom.
Is long-lit pink votives giving up on a lonely altar.
Is when a pack of mental voices funnels to one, or
    two, or—
Is when you stop counting.

For Lent, I will give up going to church.
I remember all the parish halls and community annexes
where you'd go afterwards
for egg sandwiches and glazed donut holes.
The halls are being sold off around the province now
for legal fees and judgement days.
I told the Bishop I was gay over dinner one time.
He became very, very interested in his plate
and the person sitting to his right.

For Lent, I will draw up an accounting system for sins
that will tell us how to feel. Let this spreadsheet
be analyzed by a think tank of emotional economists
who double-check all their figures
and aren't drawn in by appealing numbers.
Let *them* scratch their heads at the remainder
that I can never factor into any airtight system:
what happens when you force yourself to give something up?

A decade later, I accidentally cut off
the end of my finger in design class-belated bris.
The blood Dalmatianed the white floor
and the only way the doctor could get it to stop
was a special gel that forced a scab to grow.
It is not available over the counter
and I believe it only works on physical wounds.

I wish I could rub some into my sorest spots tonight
while I watch the news for coverage
of the Bishop's trial.
No more First Communions.

These days, I have my own students.
On Fat Tuesday, I tell my students
to stop the clocks
on their phones.
Then they'll tie long laces
of red liquorice into necklaces
and wake up to Mardi Gras every day.

Let one candy strand fall on the floor,
come home on my boot bottom
and get treaded into my doormat.
Let me take it to the laundromat
where I will run into a friend from college.
Let me bundle up all of the words of the hidden affair
like a warm pile of dryer-sheet socks
and drop them at my friend's feet.

Let me tell my old friend
that I slept with our professor
who had said, at the end,
*This would really hurt you
if it ever got out.*

# EATING CHINESE IN KINGSTON, NOVA SCOTIA (POPULATION: 5174)

*Sweet and sour pork has always been on the menu. It has always tasted like this. It always will...[Its] story functions as... the genesis of fake Chinese food. It would be the story of the creation of Chineseness specifically for Western consumption...The story of sweet and sour pork suggests the creation and circulation of a Chineseness that is a substitute for the authentic, timeless, and unchanging other of settler colonial consuming desires.*
—Lily Cho, *Eating Chinese: Culture on the Menu in Small-Town Canada*

"Oh, I don't actually *eat* this stuff,"
the waitress responds to my question of
"what's *your* favourite dish?"
(Her word is "stuff" but the intonation is "shit.")
Then: "I take it you're an expert?"
Gum snaps, I stammer. Mom smiles.

Bao Loc: where piercings and pink shirt
read as urban attitude,
where a fat food-lover tries,
gingerly, to order light,

where the white waitress
must bring peanut butter sandwiches
for dinner each night.

It reopened this week with new management,
new paint, one new menu item.
We hem and haw, Mom and me,
but go for the new one: "the pad thai, please."

The one Thai supplement to the maple-leafed
catalogue of Chinese:
       onion rings, fluorescent-sauced meat,
       perennially sweet but never actually sour.
       We wait half an hour for egg rolls
       while the new owners pace, sweat, stare.

       We're in Kingston, where the highway exit
       and entrance are on opposite sides of town.
       A tourism strategy or a warning to kid queers:
       *to get out, you've got to go through.*
       Must drive past Bao Loc, must drive past
       two-ton statue of a bull with balls.

Last week we bought pork belly
from the farm up the old road.
Bulk-buying pork is kosher in a town
where the civic festival is a cow roast.

(Three cows, actually—
and the one that leads the festival parade
never sees it coming.)

Bao Loc used to be called Me Kong.
Fried rice, battered chicken, curtained VLTs.
Before that, it was an apartment. The side door
has a screen and is tied shut with rope.
    The owner of our village's non-chain grocery store
    hung himself in 2003, between his local apples

  and the bananas. It's dog eat dog
  and the new Sobeys carries fish sauce
  (though this pad thai has none).
  It has lime, soy, and more than enough sugar

  to candy-coat the unknown truths
  about what life might be like off the grid
  of the old Acadian Lines bus routes.

  Out there, people think they already know us.
  But this place and these noodles withhold
    like empty fortune cookies
    held to the ear to hear the ocean.

# MY FATTEST AUNT

went through our back deck, but just one leg's worth.
This leg dangled in the deck's dark underbelly,
where the black cat would go in a thunderstorm,
where only the bug-brave would hide
when others were seeking.
The rest of her was left on deck,
applying the pressure of her pounds
to a ring around her thigh.
Later it bruised first-degree purple,
shame-shade of a varicose vein gone feral.
The toes that led the leg's way through the wood
did not reach the ground. They sought earth,
craved gravity to help bear the load. My mother,
like an adrenalized logger
who deadlifts a timbered trunk from a toe,
tore the siding off the deck, crawled under, and built a
tower of stones
under my aunt's foot, bringing her down to earth
by raising the earth up to meet her.

My fattest aunt is at odds with her world.

She taught me lessons:
How to love imported salami bought on credit.
How to deal with adults throwing tantrums.
That fat falls but floats.

One day, she'll push herself
up through the soil
as a cat's cradle of roots.
No, it won't be soon,
and I can't tell you how I know.

# PLEASE DON'T BURY ME DOWN
# IN THAT COLD, COLD GROUND

*No, I'd rather have 'em cut me up.*
*And pass me all around.*—John Prine

Use my tripe for dental floss;
Transgender women can have my tits.
Braise my ribs in honey-garlic sauce;
Burn my slick pits, zits, and clit.

Use my temper to dispense with folks
Who always get stuck in your craw.
Daddy-dutch, don't you ditch my yolks—
The finest hollandaise you ever saw.

Duck, duck, goose, get my liver to Quebec;
Chefs, it's almost foie gras.
Tartar my tongue, make a broth with my neck,
Then, baby, choke me down raw.

Use my calluses to sand down your edges,
Use my butt to make some soap.
If you're hungry for change then dredge,
Batter, fry, and eat my cunt for hope.

Puree my asshole into wieners;
You know people love that shit.
When the bread's broken, be Catholic keeners
And consecrate a whole vat of my spit.

Salvage my piercings and store in a Ziploc bag,
Give them away to someone unsuspecting for free.
Wring out my favourite shorts for my guerrilla rag
And institute a bloody archive of mouldy me.

Take my offbeat heart to the clock shop,
Throw 'em all off for years.
Tenderize my loins, shellac my chops,
Donate my funhouse mirrors to my queers.

Feed my yeast to brew your beers
(At least something is still alive).
Rub my grease on a few good steers,
Remember rosemary, thyme, and chive.

Grind my milk-bones for *Titus Andronicus* pie.
Serve with crumpets and a spot of pee.
Tan and treat my thick-skin hide;
Quill my blood to write your new treaty.

Play your soundtrack on my vertebrae xylophone
(To hell with cell-phone style).
Ignite my gas before a zealot's home,
Extinguish it with my pool of black bile.

My feet were made for more than walking;
Don't waste the years I spent on that gut.
Repurpose my chins as makeshift caulking
To seal this casket shut.

> But, please don't bury me
> Down in that cold, cold ground.
> I'd rather have 'em cut me up.
> And pass me all around.

# ONE OF MY THIN FRIENDS

You don't know embarrassment until somebody has tried to fuck you in one of your fat folds, and of course I mean embarrassment for the other party and not myself. I felt bad for that person, but only because we were on camera. Can you imagine being documented for life as someone who couldn't find the cunt of a morbid o-beast? Wouldn't you just *die*? Wouldn't you just curl up under a fat comforter with a fat teddy bear and watch some fat porn in order to study up and to shame-masturbate while you cry over your thin-minded folly? As for the person who truly did lose their dignity thus, I believe the half-rotten zucchinis helped their case somewhat. Yes, they could blame it on the produce: *Hey, YOU try getting it in the right place when the fucking implement you are using in that particular moment is neither sentient nor firm!* Indeed, I think much of the debacle can be blamed on agriculture, like many bad fucks or even medium-quality fucks. The frat boys don't call it getting corn-holed for nothing. It's because corn is a fucking disgusting food. Oh, my professor friend teaches some dumb article about frat boys—how they tell jokes about how to find fat women's vaginas. The joke has something to do with coating them in flour, or breading them—something that reminded me of fried chicken. All I took from it is that guys secretly love fucking fat people, but only in secret. Like, I had a skinny roommate who said his favourite dinner was a tie between coquilles St. Jacques and a deconstructed Steak Oscar with rapeseed-oil aioli even though I once walked in on him at night because I thought he was having a nightmare but he was just tummy-down on his bed mashing his face into a bag of Cheetos and grunting. Now, that metaphor doesn't quite work, so don't quote me, because it implies that fat people are of lower nutritional value or whatever the sex equivalent of that would be. That is untrue. Some of us are so highly nutritious that we fuck and eat zucchinis, you know. Or was it a cucumber? What I wouldn't do for some tzatziki and grilled meats right now. There was no meat at the party where the fold-fucking faux pas occurred, only very small oranges and a bottle of maple syrup that was eventually poured atop someone from England, as per her request. Nobody asked if she was a crêpe or a crumpet. But as for my thin friend, my fat-fucking strumpet, well, I loved that person so. We remain the best of buddies. But I'll never ask that friend over for crudités. That would just be cruel.

# CHAIRS AND STAGES CAN'T CONTAIN ME

I.
I sublet a condo from a retired civil servant in Montreal.
I put away all his unnamable animal rugs.
Only accidentally did I see his photo album
of him and his former lover. AIDS.

The legs of his chairs slowly unhinged
under me over the year.
I superglued everything back together again.
He invites me over for dinner now that I've moved out.
I nightmare a scene of lumbering musical chairs,
which turns into a game of fatso Russian roulette that I win.

II.
After a Pride Parade, my performance troupe
danced at the public square for thousands.
Gave those Vanilla Ice moves all my swagger-sweat.
They had to pause the show afterwards
because the surrogate stage (oh, plywood,
you'll be the death of a fatty)
came unhinged in just my corner.
Sucked on my inhaler all day;
venison sandwich with a lover;
danced until morning.

III.
I stood on an old wooden stage in the Rockies
tightrope-walking fat toes across antique timber
before skinny literati. *Well, at worst,*
*I'll have a good story one day*
*about bringing the house down in the prairies...*

# MY LAST MEAL

A cup of orange juice squeezed
between the retired pope's thighs.

A gallon of diet orange soda pop
because (aspartame haters be damned)
I'll burp *my* goodbyes.

I'll gnaw on Lloyd Robertson's kidneys, I will.
Chase them with a guava milkshake and
that assassin some would call a pink anti-depressant pill.

An enema (from) an enemy.
Another too-whipped bowl of organic cream.
Anything but another cauliflower-as-pizza-crust meme.

A Ziplock of frozen tuna tartare
to ice my burning hip.

Eggs cooked to 63 degrees,
atop ropy cheap beef cheeks.

More cheese

Mom's tuna noodle bake

Jamón ibérico and
champagne (no fakes)

More gristle
More salt

No sweat
No wake

# FAILED SEANCES FOR
# RITA MACNEIL (1944–2013)

I.
Rita, you requested that your ashes
be held in a teapot—two if necessary, you said.
> Low days, I browse plus-size caskets
> (They are all pink or blue)
>> But you took death with
>> milk and sugar, long steep.

Rita, we are both members
of the fat neo-Scottish diaspora.
> Don't tell me it doesn't exist, sweet darlin',
> until you are the only fat transsexual
> at a Rankin Family concert in Montreal.
> Until you feel more at home
> than you have all year when
> Raylene (1960–2012)
> thumbs-ups your half-ton dance moves in the front
> row during that last last encore.

> *Fare thee well, love.*
> *Will we never meet again no more?*

II.
In Grade Two, I sang with your coalmining choir,
The Men of the Deep. There is something terrifying
about a hundred prepubescent squirts
squeaking out the high falsetto tones of "We Rise Again"
over the miners' sea of capsized bass tones. The highest note

of the song comes at the word "child" and we screamed it.
We didn't yet have the sadness that keeps you
from even trying those high notes that take you
from ours to other worlds and back again.

> A miner comes forward
> in concerts for a mustachioed solo.
> He was on the CBC the day you died,
> having an open cry.
> They all wear helmets onstage.
> They are all Henny Penny,
> ever hardhat-ready for another falling sky.

Rita, did I ever tell you
my great uncle Miley died in the mines?

My mother and I drove to Glace Bay last year.
The old company houses are split
down the middle. Each half is a
different hand-painted hue
and empty.

We bowled candlepin alone in the basement of a church,
but it did not strike us to genuflect upon entry.

III.
Rita, I heard you were trailed by the RCMP in the '70s.
They weren't arts reviewers, those Mounties:

> *She's the one who composes and sings women's lib songs.*
> *A hundred sweating, uncombed women*
> *standing around*
> *in the middle of the floor with their arms around each*
> *other crying sisterhood and dancing.*

They don't know the gravitas required
of a fat woman who wants a microphone.
They didn't see you as a teenager with a baby
decades before *Juno*.

Or the surgeries you had for the cleft palate of your youth.
Not even the abuse you sang through.
They don't believe in ghosts like we do or
know those family spirits

that can refill a rum tumbler
when your back is turned.

IV.
Rita, do you remember the Heritage commercial
about the mine collapse?
An actor swears that they sang those hymns,
drank their own "you know"…
At seven, this frightened me,
but now I've seen a bit:
 I've watched Ashley MacIsaac (1975–)
 discuss urination during sex.
 I still toe-tap to his first crossover hit,
 and still watch the bit on Conan O'Brien
 when he kicks up his kilt while going commando.
 Yes, to queer kids watching at home,
 a kilt can become a portal to another life not yet
 witnessed or possible.
 *Step we gaily, on we go,*

*heel for heel and toe for toe!*
I want to feel Ashley move his bow, dab at his brow,
wash his feet or at least buy him a pedicure
so that I can tell him        the queer rural Nova
Scotian diaspora

                        (don't tell me it doesn't exist, b'y)
        needs him to survive because
                my accent is buried in Banff now
                and he's the last member of my
                trinity still (last I checked) alive.


V.
One of my fat aunts resembles you, Rita.
Once, at the liquor store, someone cried:
*I didn't know you were in town for a show!*

This aunt grabbed her rye,
drove home angry foot to floor,
had her niece pour the spirit
until the ice floated.

She is on the wagon now. Sort of.
Her niece could be a nephew, sort of.
Things change, Rita.

Rita, say anything.
Tell me we can break biscuits
with blueberries and Devonshire cream.

Tell me that you'll let pitch-free me
hum along as you sing me to sleep.

>Just don't tell me
>we didn't exist. Don't
>tell me that you don't

>*feel the same way too.*

# II.
# BEARDED LADY

# LONG TWISTED THINGS

I had never let anyone watch me
 Eat spaghetti, brush my hair, hear me urinate.
  Beside the stove, nestled like warm birds
   Juicing garlic, laughing and licking each other's tears
    Over onions. My hands in her pockets,
     She with mortar and pestle, crushing rosemary,
     Thyme.

   Bound in sheets, she laughs at the cats
    On my underwear, and wipes my face.
    *The towels probably smell like me by now.*
    *Only if you really bury your face in them.*
     The mirror shows us to us; we're impressed
     With our volume, colour, vast contrast.
      My hair left on the pillow
       Pseudo-pubes if you didn't know better,
       Signatures.

    *Hey.*
    *Hi.*
      Curt nods, walking on, I read her body.
       Site of scrawlings, I'm cited on her toes. Footnote.
       I carry her around. She stomps atop me.
        Hoping she'll never wear sandals
         Wondering if she saw my watched wrist
          My wits nitpick our days,
           Untwining knots,
            Pulling.

# INTRODUCING THE LETTER EX (1)

My girlfriend and I are unfortunately faithful
to big pharma; we take the same
birth control pill.

My girlfriend has a name: Gone.
I have a name: glad.
Some days I wanted to tell her: *go fly a kite!*

Then she'd have been Gone, with the wind.
And quite frankly, my dear, you're still wrong
if you think I give a damn.

## SCAR TISSUE LOOKS GOOD
## ON POMQUET BEACH
*for B.*

*I can only go in up to my nipples*, I warn;
they're freshly lanced, still leaking.

Campfires here witness the stealth sex
of people passing through
on their way to the Cabot Trail. But it's in the plain sight
of hot daylight that we two transgender guys disrobe
to air out wounds and wind tales.
His nipples are like scar tissue;
he moved too much, too fast, post-surgery.

> (Rum-clumsy in a stranger's bathroom, I once
> watched my lover dot her chest with cover-up,
> dabbing red pre-pimples mid-party. The world's
> strangest bingo that in this moment strikes me as
> charmingly Martian.)

A shallow pool holds a hot population of jellyfish,
which we sit down to meet. One is inside out but
what can we do? *They've got no brains—they're like amoebas.*
A baby almost shimmies up my shorts and five big ones
are pinned down dry on the shore by three rocks each.

> Later I read that jellyfish never die; they death-defy

by morphing back into cystic blobs and starting over.
Before we shake out sand and drive back, I march in once
more with keen cold feet since the last dip
ought to be deepest.

We'll slip into the poetry reading late,
Scottish-sunburned, smelling
of salty pina coladas and few could guess why we're in
stitches.

I'll take off for Montreal,
meet a Westerner named Laura
who tells me she spent a day in Antigonish
and got a ticket
for parking in the priest's spot
in an otherwise empty lot.
She asks: *How could you stand living in a wee town
where nothing interesting ever happens?*

# AIRPLANE LAVATORY ALGEBRA

If X = my ass
and my ass is 100 feet behind first class,
then let Y be the compression required
to have X in the airplane lavatory—
I am the reluctant engineer of the Mile Wide Club.

If V = the volume of the airplane lavatory
and C = the circumference of my thighs,
then let B be the rotational axis
around which I must pivot to pee.
Like Superman, this booth transforms me—
into the lead contortionist of the Cirque de So-Gay.

If my buzz cut seatmate's hair = $A^2$
it remains unfair, this space between our chairs,
where the armrest is owned
by the acute-angled elbow he digs into me
while my flabby forearm hovers (rather non-
aerodynamically).
My god, dude, would touching elbows
be like butt-fucking me?
(Am I the first-ever fat flight attendant of Flight AC 693?)

If H = the height of the lady attendant's bangs
then P = her hunger pangs this year.

If my queer chest, uni-boobed, may be called $Q^3$
then my bad mood will be visited upon all the rubes
who own the airplane seatbelt-making factory.
They need to think bigger. Because,
at this height, I can't summon Houdini's powers
to extend the length of this bruising constraint.

Inner monologue:
*Don't worry, you'll be fine, you'll be fine, you'll be fine—*

The PA:
*Please return to your seats,
as the captain has switched on the Fasten Seatbelt sign.*

Inner monologue:
*You're still fine, you're still fine—*

Seatmate:
*The armrest is mine, it's mine, it's mine…It's mine!*

F = my fear
that *in the unlikely event of an emergency landing over water*
the others will grab me to float.
I'll kick them off with aquafit quads;
let the rich drown with their lead-rod lean bods.
Unlike the airlines, my policy is no fuss:
Noah saved pairs and I'll save 2XLs and plus.

I'm flying to a city where Fat $\geq$ just one.
It has a street of strip clubs flanked by Addition Elles,
where XXX meets XXXL.

Hell, I'm a regular Fat Elvis
entering my Graceland,
bananas in pockets,
peanut butter in hand.

# INTRODUCING THE LETTER EX (2)

I.
Before you left,
we looped a
string
around your clit,
tied it to my bits,
and stretched it
across the river.

Now I strum that
string slowly
each time I
remember.

Shall we cope
with break-up
texts that hang
in cyber-air like
dirty tropes
on a rope?

II.
I'll throw myself
a lifesaver strand
of cologne-
branded shirts
knotted together
and swing off
to join the circus.
You'll see.

No tightrope for
me. I'd choke
on a breath mint
mid-air.

I'd have the
freshest breath at
the funeral home
and the whitest
hair.

III.
If you're certain
then leave, nod
goodbye.
Tie some twine
from your coast
to mine, knowing
that when it gets
taut, one
of us is having
thoughts of
better times.
That or there's a
sucker-smoked
salmon or cod
that got caught
capered on the
line.

# O, ADULTHOOD

Aloof fools choose gloomy bedroom afternoons—
noose-hooked selfhood, looped too loose. Crooks
loot backdoor bankbooks. Newsroom onlookers *ooh*.
Reboot. Barstool goofs spook too soon. Moody goons
co-op schmooze. Broods spoon-feed food, cooing.
Boozed groomsmen booty-woo. Surefooted tattooists
shoot moons—boomerang hooves boot bamboo
floors. Soundproof rooms cook smooth booming
subwoofers, woodblock, kazoo, spoons, blueblood
bassoon. Books soothe, books flood Chinook-shook
roots. Books spoof stoolpigeon tycoons. Marooned
bookworms mooch scooped-up Saskatoons.
Photooxidized cocoon—*Goodbye, moot soot.*

## THE FORCE REQUIRED TO OCCUPY MY
## SHIRT IS STRONGER THAN GRAVITY

I'm making my chest a Community Chest.
I had both nipples pierced with blue barbells,
doffed my shirt for a rapt punk piercer who said:
*Ok, you're transgender, but what will you do for a wiener?*
Walked home on the strength of a granola bar,
watched as the blood set, encasing each nipple
like those pistachios they dye red.

YOU HAVE WON SECOND
PRIZE IN A BEAUTY CONTEST—
**COLLECT $10**

I'm making my chest a Community Chest.
I had both nipples tugged by a lover
when I had a different home and name.
Once, when trimming its hairs, I sliced off a slab of breast
like the mad operator of a gothic carvery station.
I decided I'd never trim again.
The scar has the topography of a seashell.

DOCTOR'S FEES—
**PAY $50**

Everyone asks: *Did you get the surgery?*
(As if there is just one.)
I've known no knives, and it may surprise you
that this seems to disappoint people
because I'm not like that person you know from TV.
These dramas are so many microscopic bed-bug motels or
parasites that park on the boulevard of my chest.

YOU ARE ASSESSED FOR
STREET REPAIRS—
**$40 PER HOUSE**

I build skyscrapers out of cotton batting on Electric Avenue.
I poledance in zero gravity with a scaffolding beam.
I disinter an Emerald City bank buried in a flood.
I retrofit jails into red-sequin-shoe mirages.
You could join me off the map
if you knew how to take a

**CHANCE**

# INTRODUCING THE LETTER EX (3)

I don't believe
in giving advice but
I can tell you
that answering a personal ad
from someone seeking someone
who wants to stomp
across your back
in their fiercest spike heels
while naked *is*
as bad an idea as it seems.

# MONOGAMY
## (A LOST LETTER FOR READING ALOUD)

*Dearest, I love you!*
  When I hear your name, my mind projects
  beautiful images:  roses, laughter, wide eyes
  highs and lows, and blueberry pies a la mode.
  You and your cousin in disguise as guys
  at a seedy bar where you'd both take it too far
  flirting with me, creep into the men's washroom
  and reach so deep into me that your hand
  unfurls out of my mouth and waves goodbye
  as I come and we go. No, so far into me that
  if I did my Kegel crunches each day
  I could contract like a vice grip and
  amputate your hand at the wrist,
  at the wrist as though you're a thief,
  a thief who has stolen my heart.
  Till death do us part.

*Darling, I adore you!*
  When the phone rings, my pulse quickens
  knowing it could be you. Yes, it quickens
  to an almost sickening pace, like a vegan
  who is faced with a beer-can non-organic chicken
  and spews. Or like some mean rude dude's dude
  who chews his food, swallows, and makes a scene
  when he finds half a used tampon blitzed

into his Cherry Cheesequake Blizzard at Dairy Queen.
When the phone rings, yes, a ventricle in my heart
pumps blood harder than you pump me
with my own strap-on, which could be blue
but not nearly as blue as the oxygen-free dirty blood
that takes a trip around my body and comes back
to the ventricle in my heart
and not nearly as blue as I am
when I am without you.

*Baby, I do want to be with you till death parts us!*
    From start to end, on the mend
and in health, I'll always be parked
at your bedside.
If one day you died,
and I cried, I'd take pride in
watching you 'sleep' with that weird
sewed-up smile at your wake.
I'll pat your fat ass in the casket
and scorn the fake tears of basket case
chatty taskmasters who never knew
which bodies mattered. I'd be flattered
if you'd let me hold your dead digits.
By then, your hand will feel like a rubber glove
made to wash dishes. Everyone else

munches on finger sandwiches
and gets drunk on holy spirits
in the other room. Because
your happiness is as ubiquitous
on my priority list as are pubic hairs
in the keyboards of public computers,
I will sneak back in after midnight
and lovingly rip open your lips
and re-stitch each stitch the funeral director
sloppily sewed because he's so depressed
that his life is nothing like *Six Feet Under*
and tomorrow he has to watch me cry.
I, who would use military-issue invisible thread
on your hell-bent death-gaping mouth
      just because to see you smile
      is that important to me.

# III.
# SWORD SWALLOWER

# ROAD RULES

I refuse to lift my middle finger to the sea foam 1996 Geo
that cuts into my father's funeral procession only to pull
a hard right into the tiny Tim Hortons a block later.

> For my driving test,
> the invigilator takes me two towns over
> to find some traffic and a stoplight,
> where I will perfect  parallel parking
> on a dirt road's cold shoulder—no other bumpers,
> just crops,
>
> and I refuse to reveal the details
> of my mother's labour board hearings,
> those stories of fired coffee-slingers
> who hyena at the word "barista"
> and feed closing-time crullers
> to regulars rather than dumpsters.

There's a seventeen-minute drive and estimated
seventeen-grand gap in income
between Exit 17 and Exit 15. Berwick is to Kingston as
picket fence is to picket line,
as tight lips are to stiff upper ones, as bills are to change.

When I've buried god, my mother
will still cross holy water on my knee
before any drive longer than an hour.

Parched on a Cape Breton golf course,
my sister grabs our mother's long-
left glass Snapple bottle
from the car, and after shooting a record score,
learns it was full of old holy water.

Kory and I spent study hall off-roading his Corolla down
Gay Park's grassy hill. I drove past last summer—
the tire tracks are gone and Kory is a missionary now.

I shared one mixtape with my sister
and when I hear those songs, my bones ring
like a rusty, hungry dinnertime bell.

# CANADIAN LITERATURE PREMISES

Empire: An Elegy

The Gosling Glosas

The Road Not Plowed

The Ghomeshi Sestinas

I Kissed the Cod and I Liked It

Pour Some Maple Sugar On Me

The Affair I Considered Having Once

Do Not Go Gentle Into That -40°C Night

I Wandered Lonely as a Habs Fan in Toronto

Beaver Also Means Vulva and I Am Not Creative

The Day That You Googled "vulva versus vagina?"

What If Tim Horton Hated Donuts? An Epistolary Novel

Roughing It in the Bush: An Anti-Colonial Lesbian Rewrite

Trees and Birds Are Extremely Moral: Variations on a Theme

The Terrain Reflects my Struggle Yet Again, and Other Poems

The Weather Mirrors my Mood Once More, and Other
Ways I'm God

Who Would Top If Justin Bieber and Rob Ford Hooked
Up: A Pantoum

Dan Aykroyd's Disgusting Goddamn Vodka Would Be
Improved by Tang

Something My Mother Handed Down to Me Makes Me
Think Anew of My Children

Dear Childhood Friend Who Drowned in a Grain Heap:
My Life Has Been Hard Too

The Ocean is Very Vast and When I Think About It,
Small Seas Drop from My Eyes

Each Ring of This Majestic Maple Reminds Me
of a Wrinkle on Ashley MacIsaac's Dick

Because You [Adjusted] Me:
A Poetry Diary of Celine Dion's Jaw-Cracking Chiropractor

While Researching How a Minute Part of a Tractor Engine
Works, I Learned Something Profound About Labour
The Day I Saw Douglas Coupland Crying in Quebec
While Talking About Terry Fox and the Various
Colours of Salmon

Wilfrid Laurier Reincarnated as a Slam Poet and Step
Dancer Who Lives in Fort Mac and Performs Under
the Name 5-Dollar Will

I Pooped in the Seawater at English Bay and the
Clouded Water Represents My Hazy State of Mind Upon
Committing Such an Act of Environmental Terrorism

I Bear Some Resemblance (Both Physiognomic and
Ancestral) to Rita MacNeil, so Perhaps Somebody Would
Like to Read About My Vicarious Identifications With Her

Sonnets for Fathers Who Smell of One or More of the
Following: Tobacco, Dirt, Pine, Animals, Jerseys, Farts,
Bacon, Old Spice, Sweat, Sweatpants, or Other Manly
Things like Penises and Taints

A Prairie Lover Flew to a Conference in Montreal
With Brand New Sneakers That Had a Maple Leaf
Pattern on the Sole but Her Keeper Fell Out and She
Stepped in the Blood and Left a Red Leafy Trail
as She Ran to the Salle de Bain

A Letter to Poetry Readers Who Are Men But Who Have
Never Even Heard of a Keeper: Catch the Fuck Up, Do You
Even Know Any People Who Bleed and Are Boycotting
Tampax on the Grounds of Morality and/or Personal
Inflexibility for Insertion?

OMG I Just Had a Dream That Colonialism Became
Unfashionable and That Heterosexual Sentiment Was No
Longer Mistaken for Universal and That I Could Fly and
That Nobody Ever Went Missing and That I Was Taking
My High-School Math Exam Again but Then Suddenly
I Was In My Grandmother's House Next to a Scary Life-
Sized Statue of Infant-Jesus but Then I Awoke and There
Was a Drool Pool On My Pillowcase and No Peameal
Bacon in the Fridge for Breakfast Either: A Haiku

Atwood Mad-Libs

An Apologia

# HOMETOWN


Welcome to a hometown, where everyone knows
about the Ninja Turtles sweater
of your second-grade school photos (classy with a skirt),
your name, address, inherent hair hue,
details of your first date, first kiss, first—
and they whisperhiss about your prescriptions.

About the Ninja Turtles sweater
of your second-grade school photos (classy with a skirt)—
it might have given it away to them at age seven,
and they whisperhiss about your prescriptions:
*The Pill? I heard she was queer!*

It might have given it away to them at age seven,
trading hockey cards, sitting stocky, gawking at pogs.
*The Pill? I heard she was queer!*
The ringing refrains of rectitude.

Trading hockey cards, sitting stocky and gawking at pogs,
growing swiftly. Sifting out
the ringing refrains of rectitude
reverberating in the hollow bones of a village that snores.

Growing swiftly, sifting out
the silt of sayings and making marrow matter.
Reverberating in the hollow bones of a village that snores
and shakes its neighbourhoods awake when a character
defies the genre.

The silt of sayings and making marrow matter
materializes in worry: *a lot of those 'writers' lose their faith.*
God knows the place
shakes its neigbourhoods awake when a character
defies the genre
and squirms as if pews cause communal hemorrhoids.

Here, the 'where' wears you down,
tales taper around you, containing
your name, address, inherent hair hue,
details of your first date, first kiss, first—
*What should you do with your life?*
Welcome to a hometown, where everyone knows.

## INTRODUCING THE LETTER EX (4)

*You just slip out the back.*

I was bleeding and you
had cancer that first week.

*Make a new plan.*

We both love Frida Kahlo, but
only one of us has a unibrow.
Only one of us has a uterus.

*You don't need to be coy.*

You are desire suspended:
hopeful tyke, wormless hook.
I am an antique promise that creaks
when it's going to rain.
Your old wharf shuddered
and you mistook it for me.

*Just get yourself free.*

You don't dance,
I'm indifferent to pitch.
But some night soon
I'll drunk-karaoke-croon
for you my new cover:

*50 Things to Say When We Find*
*One Way to* [          ] *Each Other.*

## I GOT AN A+ ON THE TEST BECAUSE
## I COULDN'T STOP REREADING

In *Sociology 241: Socialization*, our text told a tale of a fat woman wedged too snuggly into a booth at Dairy Queen.

Help arrived to cut her out of the booth with a plus-size saw that could have carved many turkeys.

The textbook didn't say whether or not
the rescue workers made eye contact with her.

# INFOMERCIALS

You promised so much: apple snacks for the kids, two completely different dinners made in less than ten seconds, a sweat-free Super Bowl of dips, a turkey from frozen to table in less than an hour, that I wouldn't taste the spinach in the juice if I just mixed it with watermelon and pineapple, that I would never be messy or frustrated or counter-cluttered again, that it would pay for itself in only a few months, quick clean-up, no more ordering pizza at 11 PM, a happy family around a table thanking me for the dinner I steamed, beef jerky that was edible and delicious, fish jerky, turkey jerky, jerky jerky, banana chips, homemade Fruit Roll-Ups, healthy sausage, bouncing mounds of linguini, chopping skills, reduction of waste, flavour-lock technology, that I would stop second-guessing myself when I speak, that I would get a better job and remember my East Coast hospitality, that orgasms would come quick and easy, that I would learn how to save money or spend better or stop having to gather up change on the 26th of every month, that I would get enough of a life that I would no longer spend Sunday afternoons watching infomercials, that while doing so I would not feel a twinge of happiness when the Magic Bullet team appears on screen, that I'd stop picturing myself as the personal friend of the "lovable drunk" and "cynical senior" and "veggie-hating man" characters that you used to convince me to buy this mini-blender, that I would stop taking pills and not even notice, that I could leap across tall buildings and will myself through sheer force to grow a third hand and have the memory of an angry archivist and the hair of a recluse librarian and the cats from the best lesbian communes and the warmest quilts in winter and the least humid air in summer and that I could be many things and, like the others that promised everything just everything in a box in three just three easy payments, you have possibly let me down.

# MUZZLED

Dancing, you wrap a *keffiyeh*—Arab
headdress-cum-your-dandy-scarf—around your face
to help you resist the temptation to slip anything
unsavoury past your thin lips.

For seventy-four years, Britons who availed themselves
of hair powder paid tax—save for kings
and soldiers. One guinea for a man to scatter lavender-
scented starch onto his off-white wig like ashes.

We coat-closet kiss the same day that other newsworthy
events occur, both global (toy store employee trampled to
death, wars persist) and local (angry neighbours protest
loud eight-armed tryst).

Dancing, I pop a tight hip joint, flick a middle toe to the
sky and know one disco day I'll see you, your scarf down,
scarfing down sweet 'umble pie.

In a hot dungeon of naked men, your extra-small
T-shirt clings to your chest like swine-flu fever.
You count to ten and count on a bell
or prayer to save you from your swallowed self again.

Lawrence of Arabia paid a soldier to beat him with birches
for a decade—felt guilty, they say.
But have they ever felt the pleasure of a camel hump
swaying, syncopated, against

a scorched, scratched back?

# DEPRESSION

**LOW POINT #1**
out of toilet paper
pharmacy three blocks away
send help

**LOW POINT #2**
going to a Halloween sex party dressed as a teddy bear
sitting in the kitchen the whole time
politely offering everybody grapes

**LOW POINT #3**
flying to my mother's house
because I couldn't take care of myself
going nocturnal
sharing a meal
my breakfast
her dinner

**LOW POINT #4**
just asked my sister if she thinks my teddy bear still loves me;
I'm 29

## LOW POINT #5
had to hire a maid with my maxed-out credit card
she is 22 and very excited, uses a crystal as deodorant
BO definitely worse than the mess was

## LOW POINT #6
death-white sheets on the king-size bed
marked by the orange stain of my large beetle body
the result of three month's lying
on only one side

## MODEST STEP #1
ordered a very healthy smoothie from the vegan restaurant
to be delivered to my basement cave

spilled it...

...no mop

# LETTERS, IN ANY CASE

I.
Secrets are not meant to secrete. Opening legs
and mailboxes reveals the difference one letter makes.

At the infirmary, my mother wrapped stabs, pushed
pudding, witnessed suicide
by Javex java and scrubbed the blood of home remedies for
transsexuality.

Across town and time, last warnings clack through a
hospital phone line as I gulp
down squares of blond chocolate like a shoelace snake
swallowing Scrabble pieces.

II.
Forget my double-entendres from mishmashed genres,
mishaps from misshaped
mantras that high school was so fond *of*. (Sentences and
things ought not to end this way.)

With these filthy old tropes that heave me up dry-spelling.
Quelling an itch, you and a heart beat me out of time.

III.
When we learn to be amnesiacs, where will we be?
Sitting cross-legged in moonshine. Beaming,

you'll recite the alphabet
backwards into my ear.

# INTRODUCING THE LETTER EX (5)

Her favourite sweater
was five years my senior.

Wouldn't someone with
this patchouli-putrid relic
made holey in the cuffs by
the burrowing of nervous thumbs
know how to hang onto people and things? No.

    Earlier today, I tied her loose sweater strand
    to a rogue nail on her railing, so as she ran
    from me she unraveled, spun yarns
    around her tripping toes and tongue.

    I still have a decade until
    I'm as old as she was then.
    3652 days to break in,
    and outgrow, *this*
    raspberry, cashmere,
    plus-size, on sale,
    V-neck number.
    Yes.

# THE HAND UNLEARNS TO TOUCH

Your palm skinning me
Running itself hunter-hand
Between the hide of my sky T-shirt
And the sick sleek of me
You said you thought I would run away
Like a cat you were petting wrong

How the hand unlearns to touch
How a sad membrane seals it up (numb glove)
How we become allergic to our own skin (dumb love)
The hand remembers the bayou-sharp snap of a *no*
And the tightrope-strain of a *yes*
Sometimes, my own hand on my chest
Feels like a paddle
A long-distance defibrillator
We have dummy hands only, voices thrown
We speak from the sides of our mouths
For this, puppets are no longer required

One week after you skin me
I walk past a fleet of hearses
At the funeral home that once
Umbrellaed me from summer thunder
A group of people stands in the parking lot
Watching the black car slip from sight
They wave in unison, big happy arcs
As if clearing the air of so much vermin
Tell me, now, how their hands can wave without weight
Tell me to whom they wave and if it is you
Tell me where you are going

And why you didn't will yourself, as ash,
Buried into the tangle-busted dusty pelts of me

# CRUISING UTOPIA

*One of the things one risks when one talks of ghosts is the*
*charge of ignoring the living, the real, and the material.*
—Jose Esteban Munoz, *Cruising Utopia*

There is nothing more perfect than a dead lover—
one who you never even had to meet, who never
held you up or pushed you down and who never once
was too bored or too busy or too    too        too

Ghosts are perfect lovers because
you don't need to clean up afterwards.
Even your hands don't get dirty
and I know you like that—all the better to  to  to

cyber-flirt and chug a virgin pina colada.
I read a pamphlet about the Olympics and it turns out
that nostalgia is London 2012's official sport,
sport. And you know you're golden.

Ghost-love gives you permission to wallow, to never
have to think whether to swallow or spit angry syllables
or cum in their face when a lover's
wrestling match goes awry.

If a gay ghost is your lover, you don't have to try
to tease a future out of the ruins. You just pitch a tent
with a nightlight under the jungle gym,
pretend you're still in Grade Seven
and jerk yourself through the sheen of him
to whom you sing.

This is masturbation with
the tool of false memories.
This is auto-fellatio without ever
having to open your mouth and speak.

Yet there is some cloud of a man
I see sometimes. I don't know
if he has been born yet or if he will be
born. I chase him—all I can do is chase him

around Alphabet City and shout: Where are you going?
Once he spat back an answer and I saw the words
manifest in the air in alphabet noodles:
THE BEST PLACE: NO PLACE AT ALL.

People say they hear blowjob moans down by
the pier, but he doesn't have any time for that.
He's off somewhere new. He doesn't
leave anything behind.

He has a gigantic knapsack that grows
each time I look at him. It's too heavy.
He pops pain pills and his spine is sloped
like Citadel Hill.

He never walks backwards, even though
he turned that one time. He is not Orpheus.
He never looked at me, but it's fair to say
I could play the queer queen Eurydice.
Whatever the cast,
the stage direction reads:
*Carry the past on your back but*
*don't turn back—*
which isn't to say
you ought not to
sometimes turn
away—
because it is a grey-grim sky that
greets us on the High Line today.

# DEAR MRS. LUBERTO

You were wrong about me.

Eleventh Grade we read *Lord of the Flies*.
You dared to read Simon's death to our invincible minds
in your lilt that made even murder a sad song.

      I ran from the room.

Later you said, *you have a gentle heart.*
You petted my shoulder with your palm.
Calm, I nodded with no words.

      I handed in my *Romeo and Juliet*
      project in a rectangular box
      It was spray-painted silver and marked
      with "Montague" like a grave.

You figured I rummaged through
all the Valley's bulk food stores
to find rosemary to glue to the top of my faux sepulchre
but those long dry twigs, I had
saved them from a funeral ham.

You thought I loved Shakespeare and I did—
not for his prolific penmanship, not his
iambic pentameter, not the multiple-choice tests
that probably turned him in his tomb.
No, I was a starr-cross'd lover
       an insomniac in a second-best bed
       sitting in calculus class studying reciprocity
       and wondering if such a thing could exist
       on the queer backroads of my province.

You admired K. and I, but we were
a stick sharpened at both ends,
a plague to both our houses,
a video-loop of a handkerchief
dropped down a flight of spiral stairs.

You thought I feared your toasted-brown retriever
and his teeth.
What I really wanted was his snout steered from my crotch
much as I'd have liked someone
to find my disappearing period.

You sometimes said my papers were very *wordy*.
When Dad died, you said I'd be okay.
You thought that being a teacher
would break my tender heart.
You thought I ran from the room with emotion.

> *Mrs. Luberto, you were wrong about me!*
> I never told you I ran from the room
> with severe diarrhea.
> I tried to tell you it was just a painted box.
> I learned that no grey rectangle is.
> I tried to say that my heart could withstand a lot!
>  Maybe I was wrong...
> I tried to send you a letter
> to show that I'm not wordy.

> It got too long.

# ACKNOWLEDGEMENTS

I cannot overstate my appreciation for the excellent work done by my editor Leigh Nash, and by Megan Fildes and Robbie MacGregor at Invisible Publishing. I thank Jeanette Lynes, whose early encouragement and teaching made all the difference.

I thank my fellow writers who attended the Banff Centre Writing Studio in 2012, especially residency mentors Karen Solie, Tim Bowling, and Tim Lilburn. I thank donors to this program and the Banff Centre staff.

I thank Jon Paul Fiorentino at Matrix Magazine for making the Robert Kroetsch Award for Innovative Poetry possible.

I thank Diane Mondor, whose tender insights helped me write my favourite pieces in the book.

I thank everyone at Canadian Women in the Literary Arts (CWILA) for the support, for all of the work that you do, and
for your transgender/queer sensibilities.

I would like to say an extra-loud thank you to all of the event organizers and curators who have invited me to perform or read over the years. Your efforts are remembered.

I thank my friends for their provocations, their art, and their support. I'd like to single out a few Alberta friends who read parts of the manuscript or provided key inspirations and collaborations: Derek Warwick, Rebecca Fredrickson, Megan Morman, Janis Ledwell-Hunt, Alex Bailey, Alanna Chelmick, Allison Karch, Norah Bowman, and Marco Katz Montiel. Thank you, Edmonton audiences, for coming to the shows.

A few of these poems began a long time ago in Antigonish, NS. I thank Paul Landry and Jenn Laudadio for their friendship then and now.

I send my love and colossal thanks to Carmen Ellison, Jen Crawford, Joan Crawford, and my aunts.

Early versions of some of these poems have appeared in *The Nashwaak Review, Other Voices, The Antigonish Review, PRISM International, Room, Rattle, Rampike,* and *Between: New Gay Poetry* by Chelsea Editions. I thank the editors and readers of these fine publications.

**SNARE**

THE SNARE IMPRINT is home to exceptional, experimental poetry and prose. It represents part of Invisible Publishing's ongoing committment to a culture and tradition of literary innovation in Canada.

If you'd like to know more, please get in touch: **info@invisiblepublishing.com**

Invisible Publishing
Halifax & Toronto

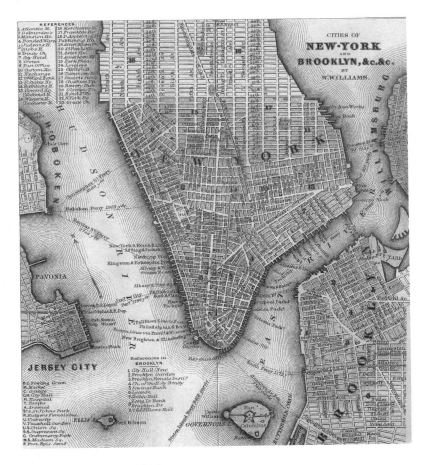

An 1847 map of lower Manhattan.

Published by The History Press
Charleston, SC 29403
www.historypress.net

Copyright © 2009 by Eric Ferrara
All rights reserved

Images are courtesy of the author unless otherwise noted.

First published 2009

Manufactured in the United States

ISBN 978.1.59629.677.0

Library of Congress CIP data applied for.

# A GUIDE to GANGSTERS, MURDERERS AND WEIRDOS OF NEW YORK CITY'S LOWER EAST SIDE

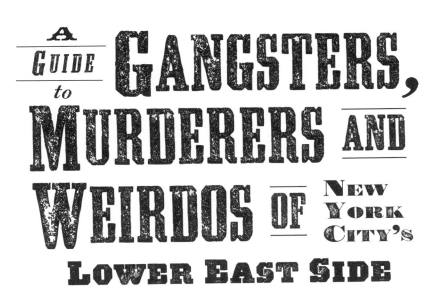

ERIC FERRARA

WITH A FOREWORD BY ROB HOLLANDER

Charleston London

THE
History
PRESS

An 1827 map of lower Manhattan.

# CONTENTS

Foreword, by Rob Hollander, PhD      7

Preface      13

Worth Street to Canal Street: A Brave New World      19

Canal Street to Delancey Street: The American Dream      65

Delancey Street to East Houston Street:
   The Promised Land      93

East Houston Street to East Fourteenth Street:
   A Radical New Direction      115

Bibliography      189

# FOREWORD

A typical guidebook is filled with the names of men and women, justly famous or unjustly obscure, whose talent, energy or genius has bequeathed lasting contributions to the social good or the cultural trove. The sites of their great accomplishments and even their homes and humble birthplaces leave a legacy of pride, ennobling our historical memory.

Not this guidebook.

Murder, mob hits, riots, rumbles, bombings and even cannibalism are the events commemorated in the streets of the Lower East Side. You'll see the shift from the Irish political gangs to the Jewish union racketeers and the Italian extortionist rings and finally a return to political violence in the countercultural East Village; all along the way, you'll experience the violence of the desperate marginal edge of social order. The story begins with the gangs.

The relationship of the nineteenth-century gangs to the city's politics reflects the broad history of post-Revolutionary New York and its emergence in the twentieth century, after one hundred years of struggle, as a progressive vanguard for the nation. Early nineteenth-century New York was a world in rapid transition toward industrialization, succumbing to the depressed wages and social instability that industrialization brings. Pre-Revolutionary New York had been a wealthy port, with a stable, if uneven, social fabric of lavishly aristocratic landowners surrounded by modest artisans and "mechanics," the highly skilled laborers who, through the traditional artisanal guild systems, regulated prices and wages. It wasn't always smooth, but it was a kind of communal society—albeit with an extravagant top end—tacitly governed by a communal ethic, with a grousing recognition from the heights that no part of an integral society could be entirely neglected.

When industrialization arrived, it marched over New York with little regard for the city's quaint integrity. Industrialists quickly saw the advantage of unskilled labor over these high-cost craft masters supporting their live-in apprentices. Industry needed a limitless source of such labor to replace the artisan and drive wages down. That source was handily offered by the tens of thousands of impoverished and desperate immigrants flooding the New York port in search of a start at the very bottom. And that's exactly what those immigrants got, although the bottom had dropped much lower than anyone had ever thought possible.

This was the context of immigrant life: housing without running water or toilet facilities (the toilet was a ditch in the backyard), no sewage system, streets piled with garbage, pigs the immigrants couldn't afford to feed running wild in the streets alongside the thousands of abandoned children the immigrants also couldn't afford to feed and prostitutes—prostitutes walking the streets, prostitutes waiting in the doorways, prostitutes reclining on the steps, prostitutes everywhere. It was estimated that one-third of the female population of New York in 1840 was or had been engaged in prostitution. And no surprise: a seamstress might earn between one and two dollars a week, working sixteen hours a day, seven days a week; a prostitute could earn nearly twice that in a day. Every second or third house in Five Points had an accommodation for prostitution of some kind. Nearly every building on Anthony Street between Centre and Orange housed a bordello.

If prostitution was nearly everywhere, alcohol was absolutely everywhere. Every building had an accommodation for whiskey. The saloon became a center of social life in the slum. The saloon owner, a man of the people, though a few steps above in income, became the local leader—trusted, respected and relied upon.

He was equally connected to a powerful industry (liquor) and to a broad constituency (the neighborhood). He could hide a local gang member in trouble with the law; he could help him out with a small loan in a pinch. The slum invested its political strength in the saloon owner, and the list of saloon-owner power brokers in New York is a long one.

The old caucus method in New York's primaries was a gang rumble. Candidates appeared at the party hall with their gang of choice, fought and whoever was left standing after the brawl took the nomination, all possible objectors having fallen silent for the evening. Candidates employed gangs to scour the graveyards for the newly dead—they would be the voters in the next election. In one election in the Tenth Ward, there were no fewer than two thousand more voters than living inhabitants. Sly critics liked to say that Fernando Wood, the controversial Democratic mayor and champion of the working class and Irish, was elected by the unanimous vote of the dead. Repeat voting was another familiar scam. There was little risk of being caught as the polls themselves were guarded by the gangs. Wood, running for a second term, gave his police a furlough on election day, advising them not to visit the polls except to vote, and promptly drew out his Irish gangs to keep out Protestant Republican voters.

New York became a battleground between wealth and political power—on the one side the industrialist, intent on the immiseration of the immigrant to keep wages low, and on the other side, the political clout of the sheer numbers of immigrants cultivating their local favorites as candidates. Wealth had created its own worst enemy, a vast working class. The struggle played out at first in Tammany Hall graft and deadly riots but eventually gave us a successful labor movement and the New Deal.

Toward the end of the century, political clout shifted from within the residential wards to the Bowery itself, lined now with flophouses, burlesque "concert" halls, saloons, gambling parlors, beer halls, restaurants, poolrooms, theatres and sensational curiosity museums cheek by jowl with prosperous immigrant banks and insurance companies, radical labor union halls and early Marxist workingmen's associations. In its bars, Tammany sachems rubbed elbows with their working-class support, while unions organized in Bowery halls for the eight-hour day. The gangs fought over turf.

Meanwhile, the neighborhood to its east, known as the Lower East Side, became the new immigrant slum as millions of Jews and Italians filed into its tenements. Their gangs now took the place of the old Irish and Protestant gangs as they fought over control of illegal rackets. Legitimate political control of the city now belonged to the Irish, the underworld to the new immigrants, and the role of the gang evolved closer to the Prohibition-era bootlegger and racketeer who still inhabit our television series and costume dramas.

Throughout these demographic shifts, the anarchism and avant-gardism of the immigrant ghetto survived, not only in the political and social radicalism of the 1950s and '60s but in the arts as well. It is no coincidence that murals, graffiti and blacksmithing grew and thrived in this slum, where the owners of private property were absent and indifferent. Scrawling and painting on an abandoned wall or welding trash into fences, arches and canopies in an abandoned lot are expressions of the fundamental anarchy that is the soul and spirit of the slum, the one space in the urban environment where the rules of property and propriety don't apply, the free space of expressive liberation for the have-nots who have only this space, the space that belongs, not to its owners, but to the people who live in it. Anarchy in its streets, anarchy in its art, anarchy in its rants, anarchy in its tenements and abandoned lots—anarchy is the slum. And the gangs, the organic order in anarchic chaos, played the crucial role, once again: it was ex–gang members who turned a Loisaida schoolhouse, abandoned by the city, into a center of the arts, Charas/El Bohio.

Since 1912, when the *Times* observed that the story of the gangs had not yet been told, many versions of nineteenth-century gang history have appeared. Asbery's *Gangs of New York*, popularized by Martin Scorsese's movie of the same name, Luc Sante's *Low Life* and Anbinder's *Five Points* all have opened up the history of gangs to public view and influenced our thinking about them to the extent that it is hard to describe the slums of New York without reiterating their stories and their perspectives. Much of what I have described here can be found in greater detail in their narratives. Books on Mafia crimes and internal warfare, hits and rackets, investigations and trials are too numerous to list in this space.

Next to those, the book you have before you is distinctly different. Not a narrative, almost a reference, it comes close to being an objective account, skewed only by its focus: violence. Eric Ferrara's compilation of disruption and murder in the slum will immediately bring to mind, to those who have seen it, the photographic work of Weegee, the freelance crime photographer who recorded, without bias or propagandistic intent, the murdered, mangled, stifled, stabbed, brutalized and bullet-ridden. Weegee's is a shocking body of images, tough and real, without the amelioration and soft filter of explanations and justifications, the diversion of armchair social theories or nods to the latest in political correctness. Like Weegee's work, Ferrara's is a cold, hard drink of fact, straight from the bottle. Grit your teeth.

Rob Hollander, PhD

# PREFACE

For me, as a fourth-generation Lower East Sider, researching and writing this book was a particularly enlightening and educational experience. After all these years of studying the history of the area, it was not until the research and production of this book that I was really given the opportunity to glimpse into the world of my ancestors.

Corruption, poverty, coercion, extortion, depression, alcoholism, illness, stress, abandonment, violence and depravity were parts of everyday life, affecting every single person one way or another on the Lower East Side. The kindest of men's morals were challenged on a regular basis, and the most evil knew no boundaries. Laboring for hours a day for pennies, only to come home and deal with the micro-politics of a neighborhood, day after day, year after year, wore one down mentally, physically and emotionally. Few escaped unscarred; many died prematurely from illness or violence.

The Lower East Side was arguably the most murderous neighborhood in the United States. What is in this book is just a thimbleful of murders, suicides, bombings, arsons and riots that shook the neighborhood in the nineteenth and twentieth centuries. Over the last two hundred years, there was a murder on almost every single property I researched—and many times there were multiple incidents in the same building throughout

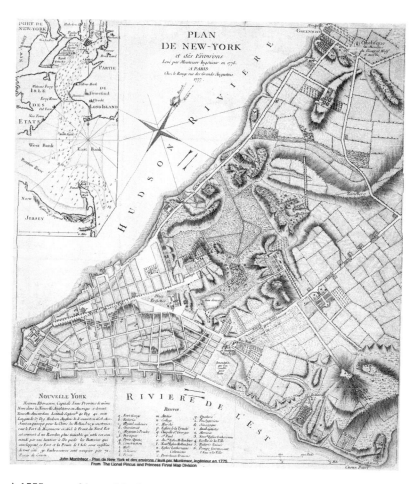

A 1777 map of lower Manhattan.

the years. Only a small and diverse handful of these stories made it into the book.

Some may say it is macabre to write such a book. I say that it is an honor to be able to memorialize the people who were victims of their times and are otherwise lost forever in history. It is stories like these that make up the bigger picture of the "melting pot" and greater immigrant experience.

This book is dedicated to my family, who survived among this craziness for over one hundred years.

The area of Manhattan covered in this book.

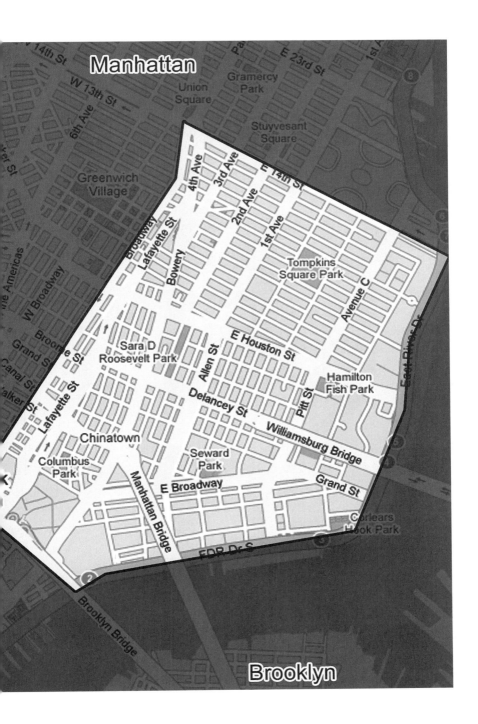

WORTH STREET TO CANAL STREET

BROADWAY
WORTH ST
CANAL ST
LAFAYETTE
CENTRE ST
FOLEY SQUARE
BAXTER ST
FIVE POINTS
MULBERRY ST
MOSCO
BAYARD ST
MOTT ST
PELL ST
ELIZABETH
DOVERS
BOWERY
E. BROADWAY
FORSYTH ST

# WORTH STREET TO CANAL STREET

## A Brave New World

Between Worth and Canal Streets, from Centre Street to the Bowery, lies the neighborhood once known as Five Points. German and Irish immigrants began to settle in Five Points as early as the 1820s. Within twenty years, it had become the foulest quarter of the young city, a vortex of pigs, prostitutes, whiskey and despair. An early slum reformer, John Griscom, prefaced his description of the neighborhood with a warning that has since entered the language: "One half of the world does not know how the other half lives." That other half lived in Five Points.

Potato blight hit Ireland in 1845, sending Irish immigrants to New York in unprecedented numbers. By 1855, close to one-quarter of the city's population was made up of Irish immigrants, over 175,000 of them. There were Germans still in the neighborhood near the outskirts, German Jews still on Baxter Street and Africans along Mosco Street and in Cow Bay, a little alley just east of Centre Street, but all the rest was Irish. They segregated themselves according to the counties in Ireland from which they hailed, joined their local gangs and fought over turf. There were businesses along the streets, and many garment makers lived and worked there, but most storefronts were groggeries or saloons, and of course, there were whorehouses around every corner. Irish girls hawked hot corn in the streets alongside the ragpickers and abandoned children.

In the 1880s, the neighborhood filled with Italians driven from southern Italy by an agrarian economic crisis. The streets of Five Points soon filled with fruit carts and organ grinders. The tenements now were taller, the neighborhood more dense and the streets more crowded. Five Points was also beginning to see the arrival of large numbers of Chinese, released from work on the railroads and no longer welcome in the West. Gambling and opium were their rackets, recessed in tunnels dug beneath the tenements, the opium so thick that you could smell it in the street. The Irish, meanwhile, had moved up in the world—their bishop now ran the archdiocese, and that included the Italian congregations; their Bowery saloon owners now ran Tammany Hall, and that included the city.

# Worth Street

Worth Street was one of the three original streets (along with Mosco and Baxter Streets) that intersected to make up Five Points. Since most of Worth Street has been redeveloped, it has been omitted from this book.

# Foley Square

You would never know it judging by the throngs of tourists strolling about and employees of the surrounding municipal buildings lunching on the park benches, but much of the blood in Five Points was shed here at Foley Square.

*Foley Square, Southeast Corner of Worth Street and Centre Street*

On August 1, 1858, a small contingent of the Bowery Boys faced off with a larger group of Dead Rabbits here at about one o'clock in the morning. The Bowery Boys were quickly overrun, and the rioters began to disperse.

Unfortunately, sixty-year-old Cornelius Rady and his son-in-law were leaving a friend's house at 66 Centre Street at the same time. The two unsuspectingly walked right into a group of raucous Rabbits, who were still riled from their war with the Bowery Boys. One of the gang members yelled, "There comes two of the Bowery Boys, let's at them!"

The gang descended on the two gentlemen. Rady's son-in-law ducked under a cart and then scurried away, escaping into the darkness. Rady started to run but was hit in the back of the head with a slingshot, knocking him to the pavement, where he lay unconscious.

The gang members ran away, and Rady was taken to the hospital, where he died of his wound shortly after being admitted. Rady lived at 109 Mulberry Street and left behind a wife and three grown children.

Patrick Gilligan was accused of the murder of Cornelius Rady, and John Quinlan, James Hines, Charles W. Gloyn and Bernard Dweyer were arrested for their involvement.

# Baxter Street

Please note that much of lower Baxter Street has been redeveloped and some of these buildings do not exist anymore, but I felt that the stories deserved to be told.

## *4 Baxter Street*

At two o'clock in the morning on June 19, 1855, shoemaker Edward McDonald woke suddenly from his sleep, procured a straight razor and slashed his sleeping wife's throat so deep from ear to ear that it sliced her windpipe and rendered her unable to cry out for help. McDonald turned himself in and was declared to have suffered from a temporary fit of insanity.

## 14 Baxter Street

On December 29, 1869, Margaret Mead was beaten to death by her own son, Michael Meade, in her apartment at this location. Michael Mead was sent to the Tombs to await trail.

Shortly after eleven o'clock at night on August 9, 1871, Polish native Joeseph Lincosta was killed in front of this address by Chinese-American resident Quimbo C. Appo, one of the earliest Chinese immigrants to New York and the city's best-known "Chinaman." Married to an Irish woman, Appo had once been held in high esteem by Anglo-Americans. This was his second murder—in his first, he had killed his landlady in a dispute; in his third, he would kill an Irishman who was beating him brutally following a card game. Appo's criminal career follows contemporary white reaction to Chinese immigration. At his first trial, many respected whites came to his defense. By his third trial, he was being called "Chinese devil-man," even though it was a clear case of self-defense. Lincosta appears to have gotten in the way of Appo's pursuit of a bunch of young toughs who had been harassing him while he slept in a doorway. As he threw a stone at them, Lincosta stepped out, receiving it in the head. At least, that's one account.

## 25 Baxter Street

"Big Tim" Sullivan, one of the most popular and influential politicians to rise out of the Irish Five Points, was raised at this address after his birth on June 23, 1863. Sullivan served during one of the most tumultuous times in New York City history—at the height of the great "melting pot" era. By the end of the nineteenth century, Italians, Slavs, Jews and Chinese were migrating by the tens of thousands and settling here, in the poor and working-class neighborhoods of the predominantly Irish and German Lower East Side. Many residents of the old Irish Five Points had moved on and "Little Italy" was born; Chinatown was emerging from the

Pell and Doyers Streets area; the German population of what we call the East Village today was replaced by the Polish and Ukrainian working class, among others; and the area just below and around Houston Street became a thriving Jewish community. To say the least, keeping order amidst all of this fluctuation was quite a task, and Sullivan was the perfect man for the job.

Young Timothy Sullivan lived in this cramped tenement building with his family, who had recently immigrated to New York City from County Kerry, Ireland. They lived on one of the dirtiest and most unsavory blocks in America and were considered to be among "the poorest of the poor" in the community.

Sullivan had to grow up quick, taking on jobs at an early age to help pick up the financial slack of his unemployed father. He began earning the respect and trust of his fellow Five Pointers as a teenager. As a newspaper delivery boy, he gained valuable contacts in the community and eventually started his own delivery business, in which he gave other poor and orphaned kids free stacks of newspapers to break into the business.

Saving enough money from his entrepreneurial endeavors, Sullivan opened the first of his four local bars on Chrystie Street. He was a charismatic, generous and trustworthy businessman, setting up fundraisers and charities for the poorest population of Five Points and hosting political events at his establishments. This altruism and good character made him so popular that he won a seat on the state assembly by the age of twenty-three. Within a few short years, Tammany Hall took notice, and by the 1890s, Tim Sullivan was the most powerful politico in Lower Manhattan, serving two terms as state senator beginning in 1894.

Tim Sullivan was a hero in the minds of the Irish Five Pointers. Unlike the great John Morrissey before him, Sullivan did not cater to outside influences for political gain. He was an outspoken, pro-Irish patriot who never caved in to pressure from "uptown" politicians. He did not drink and he did not brawl; his charisma and political power were enough to control even the most violent criminals and gangs of the Lower East Side. In fact, Sullivan is credited as being one of the first New York City public officials

to officially incorporate street gangs into politics. He recruited the
help of notorious gang leaders like Monk Eastman and Paul Kelly,
who acted as Sullivan's eyes and ears of the great vice district of
the Bowery. The Eastmans and the Five Pointers were assured the
freedom to operate unchallenged by authorities in exchange for
keeping order in the streets, workplace, saloons and gambling dens
and "influencing" voters during election time. In one example,
during the 1901 election, Sullivan hired Paul Kelly's fifteen-
hundred-strong Five Points gang to form a human chain around
local polling stations and beat back any opposition.

Sullivan made a fortune shaking down local merchants, saloon
owners and gangsters—all were required to provide a kickback in
exchange for the basic right to operate. While getting rich off of
extortion, gambling, slavery and prostitution, Sullivan also engaged
in several legitimate business ventures. He even partnered with
fellow Lower East Sider Marcus Loew, founder of Metro-Goldwyn-
Mayer pictures and Loews movie chain, in early cinema projects.

New York State senator Tim Sullivan influenced many laws in
the state, including the legalization of boxing and the passing of the
Sullivan Act in 1911 (a ploy to disarm the general public, who could
not afford the hefty registration fee, leaving Tammany goons—corrupt
police and murderous gangsters—at an advantage).

By 1911, Sullivan's life began to unravel. His wife passed away
unexpectedly after a six-week bout with tuberculosis, he lost $700,000
in savings because of his generosity and he fell ill to tertiary syphilis.
He became delusional and paranoid and was soon judged mentally
incompetent to hold office. He was removed from his senate seat and
placed in a local sanitarium by his family in September 1912.

In 1913, Sullivan escaped from the mental institution after his
guards fell asleep following a late-night card game. Tim Sullivan
never returned to the sanitarium. His body was later found near a
Westchester County freight yard in Pelham Parkway, New York, on
August 31, 1913. Sullivan's body went unclaimed for over a week,
so the city declared him a vagrant, and the body was to be buried
unceremoniously in Potter's Field. A police officer assigned to the

morgue recognized the body just in time, and a proper ceremony was arranged. Sullivan's wake took place at his headquarters on the Bowery, and his funeral was held at Old St. Patrick's Cathedral on Mott Street.

A January 11, 1866 *New York Times* article, reporting on the worst tenements in the city, singled out 25 Baxter Street, along with numbers 15 and 51 Baxter Street and 16 Mulberry Street, as some of the most miserable offenders.

Called "a hideous receptacle for human beings," 25 Baxter Street housed multiple boarding rooms in the basement, each ten by six feet with no windows or ventilation, bare stone walls and no furniture. On the first floor was a saloon that was a resort for "thieves, beggars and prostitutes of the lowest class." A local police captain stated, "I have seen as lodgers eighteen of both sexes" occupy each boarding room at a time, for which they paid about eight cents per night.

## 37½ Baxter Street

On July 30, 1859, Gibraltan immigrant Juan B. Gustarino was found bludgeoned to death in the alley at this address. It took police one year to arrest German-born Richard Bavendaun, who owned a saloon at 45 Baxter Street, in connection with the murder. It seems that Bavendaun struck Gustarino in the head with a club and robbed him as he slept in his rented room at this address. With the help of fellow neighbor Margaret Welsh, Gustarino's body was then dumped in the alleyway. The two were arrested in July 1860.

## 44 Baxter Street

In October 1875, a forty-five-year-old man, insensitively described as "a repulsive-looking colored man" named Peter Hollis, and a white woman, twenty-five-year-old Elizabeth Grumley, were arrested for "keeping a disorderly house" in the rear tenement building at this address. Grumley produced a document that stated that the two were married in 1873 at the Bowery mission, and a judge ordered

A family in a tenement room. *Photo by Jacob Riis, 1910.*

the minister who had performed the ceremony to appear in court.
Grumley was released, but Hollis was held for trial.

## 55 Baxter Street

In February 1895, Vincenzo Nino slit his wife's throat from ear to
ear after an argument in their apartment at this address. Nino was
originally pronounced insane; however, the court was not convinced
and eventually declared him mentally competent to stand trial on
first-degree murder charges.

## 59 Baxter Street

This is the site of the infamous Old Brewery of Five Points. The
building was erected in 1802 and served as a brewery until the
Irish immigration of the 1830s and '40s, when it was turned into

a boardinghouse, reportedly housing up to one thousand people at a time. In December 1852, the building was set to be demolished, but residents refused to leave. Police were called in to drag dozens of men, women and children into the streets before the building was razed to make way for the New York Missionary Society. While digging at the site, workers uncovered the bones of several Old Brewery murder and suicide victims.

### 93 Baxter Street

On January 26, 1882, a young boy was found dead in the basement of a tenement building on this site, with rats feeding off of the

"Street Arabs." *Photo by Jacob Riis.*

lifeless body. The youth had been shot in the head, the innocent victim of a shootout outside the building days earlier. After the boy fell from his wounds, somebody moved the body into the cellar, where a neighbor found him a few days later with his face and nose gnawed away by hungry rodents.

# Mosco Street

The best way to get a sense of Five Points today is to walk up Mosco Street (originally Cross Street and then Park Street). This was one of the three streets, along with Worth and Baxter, that intersected to make up the Five Points.

### 37 Mosco Street

On April 6, 1879, in true melting-pot fashion, a bloody fight between the feuding Scottish-American Lyons family and the Irish-American Kerrigan family inside this tenement building left a half dozen people severely injured. The fight started during the christening of Peter Lyons's newly delivered infant son. As the ceremony was underway, the Kerrigans, upstairs neighbors who were fully aware of the special event below them on the third floor, began stomping around so as to disrupt the festivities below. Needless to say, after an hour of their patience being tried, a contingent of Lyonses headed upstairs to confront their antagonizers. In the end, skulls were fractured, fingers were severed and blood drenched the fourth-floor hallway. All parties were treated and arrested.

### 73 Mosco Street

In the late nineteenth century, this address was home to the Ferry Room, a popular saloon owned by Italian gangster Pietro Balbo.

On August 5, 1880, twenty-three-year-old Balbo was hanged at the Tombs prison for murdering his young bride in their Rose

Street tenement apartment. The *New York Times* reported that he met his fate with "great fortitude," and "no man can ever have faced a death in a more manly fashion than did Pietro." Two days later, Balbo's funeral precession began here at the Ferry Room, and thousands of Italian Americans from all walks of life packed these narrow streets for a final farewell.

# Bayard Street

## *3 Bayard Street*

On December 23, 1883, Warsaw-born clairvoyant Anna Goldstein was attacked, robbed and nearly killed in her second-floor apartment here. Goldstein had arrived in New York City twenty-one years earlier and was considered to have made a good living "card turning" for other Polish Jews in the area. At five o'clock in the morning just two days before Christmas, Goldstein was awakened by the sounds of a Polish-Galician immigrant named Wolfen rifling through her jewelry chest. When Goldstein confronted the intruder, the man ferociously attacked the woman with a knife, stabbing and slashing her about the hands, neck, head, shoulders and legs. Goldstein was treated at a local hospital and luckily survived the ordeal, but there are no reports of Wolfen ever being apprehended. He made off with hundreds of dollars' worth of gold and cash.

## *13 Bayard Street*

A resident named Johanna Piccon was found to be listed as a patient in an infamous abortionist's diary, which was claimed as evidence in a murder trial known as the "trunk murder." Dr. Jacob Rosenzweig was accused of multiple fatalities and was finally sent to prison in 1871 for the murder of patient Alice Augusta Bowlsby of Newark, New Jersey, which he attempted to cover up by hiding the body in a trunk. The doctor spent seven years in Sing Sing before being released.

## 38 Bayard Street

On March 17, 1900, nineteen-year-old Lena Winters, a cook in the saloon that was located here, died from burns she received while working in the kitchen. Winters's dress apparently caught fire as she leaned over a stove, and in a fit of panic, the woman started running around, bumping into things and igniting several other flammable objects, setting the entire room on fire. Three people were severely burned trying to rescue Winters, and the entire apartment was destroyed.

## 45 Bayard Street

On April 24, 1887, the proprietor of a saloon at this address was arrested for murder, seven years after the incident. Back in 1879, John Smith owned a bar at 13 Oliver Street. On January 23 of that year, Smith got into a heated argument with a female patron, who yelled out for aid. Three sailors came to the woman's assistance, and Smith went upstairs to retrieve a shotgun, which he discharged, killing one of the men. Smith was convicted for the murder of Henry Madden in March 1879 but won his appeal for a new trial in November. Smith posted bail and went on with his life for seven years without being called back to trial until the district attorney reopened the case in 1887 and ordered Smith's arrest.

## 51 Bayard Street

In the early morning of December 13, 1872, Julia Smith, a lodger at the boardinghouse at this address, was killed by a man she had taken in off the streets and supported. Smith, a waitress at a "low concert" saloon on Chatham Street, had met John Harrington, well known by local police as a "perpetually unemployed ruffian and thief," only a month before he murdered her.

51 Bayard Street today.

### 83 Bayard Street

In December 1875, a man named P.N. Rubenstein murdered his wife, Sara Alexandra, in the third-floor apartment they shared. Rubenstein apparently held Alexandra down by her hair and made a quick slash with a straight razor across her throat, so as not to get blood on his hands. The murderer was captured a short time later and stood a long and harrowing trial due to contradicting witnesses. At one point, Rubenstein passed out during the testimony and had to be propped up in his seat. Eventually, the jury convicted Rubenstein, and he was hanged on March 24, 1876.

### Bowery and Bayard Street

In the summer of 1857, the gangs of New York, taking advantage of a citywide breakdown of New York City's police force, went on

Bayard Street tenement lodgers. *Photo by Jacob Riis.*

a murderous rampage through the streets of Manhattan, sparking
one of the bloodiest riots in New York City history.

In May 1857, in the midst of a political clash between
Democratic New York City mayor Fernando Wood and the
Republicans in control of the state government, Wood was
ordered by the state Supreme Court to disband the two-hundred-
year-old Municipal Police Force. Wood refused, and most of
his police officers stood by him. A newly formed Metropolitan
Police Force was commissioned by the state, and several attempts
to arrest Wood were made. These arrest attempts were met with
sincere resistance by Wood supporters, and violent skirmishes
broke out.

On the evening of July 4, 1857, a Metropolitan officer, fleeing
a crowd of angry Dead Rabbits members, ran into a Bowery
Boys saloon, chased by his pursuers. The Bowery Boys men,

The Police Riots of 1857.

incensed at this invasion of their territory by the Rabbits, and the police, intending to teach the gang members a lesson, attempted to march into the heart of Five Points, where the gang members and their families lived. They were met with a barrage of stones and bottles, many thrown off the roofs. The Bowery Boys men, unprepared for such an overwhelming show of force, were forced to withdraw until the Atlantic Guards and other allies arrived and joined in the fray.

At this intersection of Bowery and Bayard Street, hundreds of gang members and their allies went to war with hatchets, knives, clubs, paving stones, guns and just about every object imaginable. Police reinforcements were beaten back, and the rumble carried on for nearly two days, each side making small heroic advancements and tragic retreats back and forth along the Canal Street boundary line.

By the end of the second night of rioting, when the combatants were already exhausted, the Seventh Regiment of the National Guard was called out to assist the outnumbered authorities. The guardsmen, along with a large contingent of police officers (perhaps seeking revenge), savagely beat any and all participants until the entire crowd was dispersed. Rioters were sent scrambling down neighboring streets, into tenement buildings and alleys and onto rooftops.

At least one rioter was knocked from the roof of a building onto Baxter Street, where, while immobile with a broken skull, rival gang members began to stomp him to death.

The Police Riots of 1857 was finally put down by the end of the second night. Eight people lay dead and hundreds more injured.

The Municipal Police Force was disbanded in 1858. Fernando Wood was reelected to a second term as mayor in 1860. During this 1860–62 term, Wood, like many in New York, became a staunch supporter of the Southern Confederacy and sought to have New York secede from the United States during the Civil War.

Fernando Wood went on to serve in the House of Representatives almost consecutively from 1863 until his death at the age of sixty-nine in 1881.

Also on this corner, on September 19, 1883, a wagon driver named James Clarke became frustrated with a pedestrian named Joseph Price and threw his "car hook" at him. The object missed Price but struck a young boy named Lewis Robinson, of 84 Bayard Street, on the head, killing him.

# Doyers Street

## *7 Doyers Street*

In the early twentieth century, this building served as a popular Chinese theatre. On November 5, 1909, two On Leong Tong members were leaving the theatre when they were approached and fired upon by two members of the rival Four Brothers Society (or See Sing Tong). Unprepared, one man was shot in the chest and died on the scene. The other was shot in the hip and paralyzed for life. The gunmen escaped into the night, but this incident sparked a new and deadly war between the gangs.

## 13 Doyers Street

At the turn of the century, this building housed the Mandarin Café on the second floor. Above that were many small boarding rooms known by authorities for illicit activities like gambling, prostitution and opium use.

The Mandarin Café was owned by Giovanni de Silvio, aka Jimmy Kelly, an Eastman gang thug-for-hire who was a close ally of many powerful gangsters and corrupt politicos of the era. This was a popular hangout for guys like "Big" Jack Zelig and "Lefty Louie" Rosenweig during their war with Chick Tricker and Jack Sirocco.

By the first decade of the twentieth century, Jimmy was forced out, and the Chinese Hip Sing Tong took over the operations of the restaurant and brothel.

On July 14, 1912, Hip Sing Tong associate Hen Ken Yum was found murdered in a back room. He was shot once in the temple, twice in the heart and three times in his lower arm (as if he had tried to block the barrage of bullets). The assassin was never captured or identified.

## 20 Doyers Street

At four o'clock in the morning on July 21, 1904, local police raided this building, along with 20 and 23 Pell Street and 17, 18 and 30 Mott Street, arresting at least fifteen men for their parts in running open gambling parlors. Axes and crowbars were needed at 23 Pell Street and 18 Mott Street (where four sets of doors had to be breached), but police were surprisingly welcome at many of the other locations. Apparently, the street hawkers naively invited police to "come in and make a bet" when they arrived for the raid.

# Chatham Square

On November 14, 1862, a Hibernian Society funeral procession was parading through Chatham Square when a Third Avenue line streetcar broke the mourners' ranks instead of waiting for the parade to pass. The Irish benevolent organization members took great offense to this and "savagely assaulted" the driver, starting a small riot when bystanders came to the driver's aid. An army of police officers was called to the scene and saved the driver from serious injury.

## 4 Chatham Square

In an early example of road rage, an unidentified delivery driver was shot in the head and killed after a traffic dispute in front of this address. On the evening of January 21, 1873, Michael Nixon of 44 Baxter Street was driving his horse and wagon down the Bowery when he wished to turn onto Bayard Street to make a delivery. However, another wagon was blocking the intersection, and Nixon asked the man to move. When the second wagon driver refused to move, an argument ensued, and the two exchanged words all the way down the Bowery to this location, where Nixon pulled out a pistol and shot the stranger in broad daylight. At the time of the report, the victim had not been identified.

## 12 Chatham Square

In the 1890s, this building was home to a saloon owned by powerful Tammany Hall leader Tom Foley.

By the early 1900s, Jack Poggi and Jack Sirocco had taken over the saloon and were using it as their headquarters. On June 11, 1912, police raided the saloon in a one-hundred-man, citywide raid on various gang headquarters. Authorities were trying to quell an outbreak of violence that was terrorizing the city—no fewer than six gun battles had broken out over a ten-hour period, and police were getting desperate to stop it.

Jack Sirocco was originally a Five Points gang member. He was a top lieutenant and sponsor of up-and-coming Johnny Torrio. (Torrio later went on to sponsor Al "Scarface" Capone.) Sirocco jumped ship and joined the Eastman gang under Zwerbach's rule and quickly rose through the ranks.

# Pell Street

## *9 Pell Street*

On August 12, 1900, a gang fight in this building between a dozen members of the Hip Sing Tong and the rival Mongolian Masonic Order left one man dead. A gunshot rang out during a loud scuffle between the two factions in the hallway on the first floor. The group immediately dispersed, and Loang Kin was left dying on the floor. The gunman, Goo Wing Chung, ran into a building across the street at 8 Pell but was cornered by police on the second floor and arrested.

## *12 Pell Street*

On April 11, 1912, a Chinese musician named Don Sing was found murdered in the first-floor hallway of this building. Sing was struck with five bullets from a heavy revolver at such close range that each shot went straight through his body. Six members of the Hip Sing Tong, a Japanese man and two black men—all of the same address—were arrested for the crime. Police assumed that the incident began as a quarrel between Don Sing and Japanese neighbor Harry Haga over a white woman named Katherine "Philadelphia Kitty" Anderson. However, another theory is that Sing was believed to be a spy and was caught sneaking around the hallways trying to eavesdrop on his neighbors.

The *New York Times* reported that on November 21, 1920, three hundred sightseers, mostly American and Italian tourists, stepped from "a herd of mammoth" tour buses and filled Pell Street, seeking "a glimpse of the Far East." Within moments of the tourists' arrival, two local Chinese men ran through the crowd into a poolroom at 12 Pell Street and a gunfight erupted. Curiously, as local patrons fled the poolroom in a panic, the visiting tourists crowded in, looking to catch firsthand an authentic Chinatown experience.

## 13 Pell Street

This is the current headquarters of the Hip Sing Association, formerly the Hip Sing Tong (gang). The Hip Sing, which translates into "Combine for Success Society," was formed in the late nineteenth century in New York City, but by the mid-twentieth century it had set up operations in Chinese communities around the country. It was one of three powerful and violent organized street gangs that fought over control of Chinatown at the turn of the century. Its main rivals were the Four Brothers Society and the On Leong Tong (which still exists as the On Leong Chinese Merchants Association).

Please note, this is an active headquarters, and though the days of public saber and hatchet attacks are over, you will be made to feel very uncomfortable if you get too nosy. Also notice the other

Hip Sing clubhouse directly across the narrow street. Make no mistake, this is still their territory; out of respect, take a picture and move on.

## 21 Pell Street

This was home to powerful Hip Sing Tong leader Mock Duck at the height of his power in the early twentieth century. Mock Duck lived upstairs with his family and operated a private social club on the ground floor.

On January 5, 1912, Hip Sing Tong leader Lung You was assassinated here by members of the On Leong Tong while enjoying a game of fan-tan. The two assassins calmly walked into the parlor and fired ten shots at Lung You, striking him five times and killing him instantly before fleeing.

Mock Duck.

On August 8, 1922, national president of the Hip Sing Tong Ko Low was gunned down on the sidewalk here after leaving dinner, accompanied by two women. Fifty-two-year-old Tom Yee was arrested and admitted that he had a personal agenda for the murder—two weeks earlier he had been shot by a cousin of Ko Low and had vowed revenge.

## 30½ Pell Street

On August 22, 1906, two members of the Four Brothers Society gang were killed here. Low Gung and Lu Yo Fang were found executed inside their small three-room apartment on the third floor. This was part of a series of sensational murders that summer, born out of a bloody struggle to control Chinatown. Three days later, popular Chinese actor Ah Hong was found shot through the eye in his home at 10 Chatham Square.

## 31½ Pell Street

On December 4, 1910, two On Leong Tong members walked into Four Brothers Society members Quong Dong and Quong Fongs's restaurant supply store at this address and shot both shopkeepers to death behind the counter. One gunman fled through an alley along 35 Pell Street and the other slipped into a building on Mott Street—both assassins got away. The shooting was retaliation for an incident a few months prior when an On Leong Tong member had his right hand shot off while under police escort on Pell Street.

## 32 Pell Street

On January 24, 1906, two On Leong Tong members were killed and two injured outside this address when they were ambushed by a group of Hip Sing Tong members. About a dozen high-profile On Leong Tong members were exiting the building when the Hip Sing Tong jumped out from the alley and fired one hundred rounds of ammunition into the party. Lee Soon, cousin of On Leong Tong leader Tom Lee, was shot in the head and killed almost instantly. A businessman named Chin Ying was shot in the chest and collapsed on the sidewalk. As Ying gasped for air, three Hip Sing Tong members rushed him and "nearly shot his head right off of his shoulders."

# Mott Street

## *5 Mott Street*

On April 10, 1910, Four Brothers Society member Moy Yen exited the Port Arthur Restaurant at 8 Mott Street. As he passed this address, an On Leong Tong gunman stepped out from the doorway and shot Moy Yen in the right thigh. He fell to the street. The assailant then ran up to the wounded gangster and fired three more shots into Moy Yen's legs before running off. This assault began a four-hour coordinated shooting spree in both the New York and Philadelphia Chinatowns, initiated by the On Leong Tong. Their targets were both the Four Brothers and the Hip Sing Tongs, and in the end seven people were shot and four were killed in this murderous rampage.

## *11 Mott Street*

On July 15, 1910, fifty-five-year-old Four Brothers Society gang member Chu On was gunned down outside this address by On Leong Tong member Louis Wie. Chu On was walking by this address on his way to work when Louis Wie emerged from the doorway and fired five .38-caliber bullets into his target. Louis Wie fled via rooftop but was pursued by police and captured at 19 Mott Street, where he was hiding under the covers of a bed on the second floor.

5 Mott Street today.

11 Mott Street today.

14 Mott Street today.

## *14 Mott Street*

This building served as headquarters for the On Leong Tong, one of Chinatown's most powerful organizations (to this day). The On Leong Tong, which translates to "Protective of Good People Society," boasted over four hundred members at the turn of the century. The On Leong Tong's mission was to "protect the good who are weak from exploitation of the unscrupulous." However, the On Leong Tong was in actuality a violent and exploitive gang that used murder and intimidation to receive a kickback from almost every single dollar traded in Chinatown.

On February 12, 1900, On Leong Tong leader Tom Lee hosted a banquet here for dozens of New York City's most influential power brokers. In attendance were Tammany Hall leaders, judges, aldermen, assemblymen, police department and other city officials, the district attorney's office and other high-profile businessmen, lawyers and doctors.

Tom Lee and the On Leong Tong had actually been working with Tammany Hall for a number of years in a mutually beneficial relationship. Lee successfully turned out the Chinese vote in favor of Tammany Hall election after election, and Tammany Hall allowed Lee great freedom to run his rackets in Chinatown. In fact, in 1894, Lee was appointed deputy sheriff, commissioned by Tammany Hall under Sheriff John B. Sexton.

Under this arrangement, Tom Lee was able to almost single-handedly control the gambling, lottery and opium trade in Chinatown for nearly two decades.

## *16 Mott Street*

At the turn of the century, this address was known as Chinatown City Hall. About 1898, Chinatown's political, social and economic

16 Mott
Street today.

structures were essentially consolidated into one building at 16 Mott Street when several high-powered community and labor organizations moved in and set up headquarters here.

It is no coincidence that the Chinatown City Hall was set up right next door to the On Leong Tong headquarters. The On Leong Tong was technically a merchants' association, set up by the Chinese Consolidated Benevolent Association.

On September 12, 1909, Gum Kee was shot here when he "disrespected" the On Leong Tong during a day-long standoff with the Hip Sing Tong. By late afternoon, members of the two rival Tongs had lined their respective sides of the street, and dozens of police were called out and posted "every thirty feet or so" along Pell, Mott and Doyers Streets, in anticipation of a rumble.

Gum Kee defiantly crossed the battle line and posed in front of this building's storefront when On Leong Tong member Lee Wah took offense and shot Gum Kee in the back. Gang members scattered as police rushed in, and Lee Wah was tracked down and arrested a short time later.

## 17 Mott Street

Powerful On Leong Tong gang member Chin Len lived at this address at the turn of the century. On August 15, 1909, Len's twenty-one-year-old wife, Bow Kum, was found murdered here in her own bed, with multiple stab wounds to the heart. Poor Bow Kum was a young slave whom Chin Len supposedly purchased from a missionary in San Francisco. Len could not produce any official documents but told police that he suspected the missionary was behind the murder because it had made several threats recently, demanding the girl back. Len could not convince the authorities, however, and he was arrested and held for the murder.

### 18 Mott Street

This was the family home of the "Mayor of Chinatown," Hip Sing Tong leader Tom Lee. In January 1918, Lee passed away here of natural causes at the age of seventy-six.

### 21 Mott Street

At the turn of the century, this was the home address of prominent On Leong Tong leader Chu Fong. By day, Fong was a successful merchant, as proprietor of two large retail stores in New York City and Boston. By night, Chu Fong was a ruthless gangster with friendly ties to some of the most powerful politicians in New York City, including Mayors William Lafayette Strong and Robert Anderson Van Wyck.

### 23 Mott Street

In September 1900, twenty-six-year-old Mock Duck murdered Newark, New Jersey tailor Ah See in front of this building. Mock Duck was tried three times for the murder, but each time the jury found him innocent.

18 Mott Street today.

21 Mott Street today.

## 74 Mott Street

This was the address of James E. Kerrigan, an influential mid-nineteenth-century politician who had very close ties to the gangs of Five Points.

Kerrigan attended Fordham University briefly before enlisting in the army at age seventeen during the Mexican War. At the end of the war, Kerrigan joined the local Hose Company 14 firehouse at 14 Elizabeth Street, where he became a popular figure among the locals. He was elected to the district council in 1854, with the help of such notorious public figures as John Morrissey.

In 1855, Kerrigan was arrested and imprisoned for his part in the murder of William "the Butcher" Poole at the Stanwix Bar on Broadway but was later acquitted. During the election of 1856, Kerrigan and his supporters, known as the Molly Maguires, had a shootout with opposition supporters at the Elizabeth Street polling center. Dozens of people were injured, and Kerrigan emerged victorious in the election.

In 1857, during the Police Riots, Kerrigan provided support and shelter to anti–Fernando Wood rioters. When Wood was reelected a couple years later, Kerrigan made amends with Wood, and the two engaged in several political ventures.

Kerrigan was elected to Congress in 1860, representing much of Lower Manhattan. At the start of the Civil War, Kerrigan created the 777-man Twenty-fifth New York Volunteer Infantry, known as the Tenth Ward Rangers. His volunteer army was sent to be stationed in Virginia, but Kerrigan was court-martialed on February 21, 1862, under suspicion of supporting the Confederate cause.

## 83–85 Mott Street

This is the current headquarters of the On Leong Chinese Merchants Association, a one-hundred-year-old Chinatown organization that still has tremendous political power in the area.

83–85 Mott Street today.

# Centre Street

*Centre Street and Franklin Street, Northwest Corner*

This is the site of four notorious Tombs prisons. The original prison, officially named the Halls of Justice, was erected in 1839 and was nicknamed "the Tombs" because it was styled after ancient Egyptian architecture. With its broad, fortified walls, thick columns and pyramid-like stone steps, it was an intimidating structure and was meant to be so.

Inside was dark, with almost no natural sunlight and limited ventilation. Making it even more unpleasant, just five months after opening, the building began to sink under its own weight and the foundation cracked, causing water to stream through the walls and muddy puddles to collect on the cell floors. This provided a breeding ground for malaria-carrying mosquitoes and bacteria of all kinds, resulting in severe illnesses for many veteran watchmen and longtime inmates.

Even under these conditions, the Halls of Justice continued to process about fifty thousand inmates a year, including Confederate POWs during the Civil War, until it was finally torn down and replaced with a more sanitary facility in 1902. Along the way, countless suicides, murders and executions took place behind its walls, and it received widespread criticism for its lack of internal security and rehabilitation programs.

The first execution at the Tombs took place on January 12, 1839. Edward Colman, a black man who murdered his mixed-race wife, was hanged for his crime. Apparently, after Colman's wife abandoned him, he followed her from Philadelphia to New York City, where he slit her throat with a razor in a jealous rage on Broadway, where she worked the streets as a prostitute.

On November 18, 1842, John C. Colt, brother of revolver inventor Samuel Colt, was scheduled to be hanged here after being convicted for the murder of an associate. A 160-year-old mystery still revolves around some peculiar events that took place on that day.

First of all, Colt married a woman named Caroline Henshaw just hours before his scheduled execution. Then, a mysterious fire broke out in one of the cellblocks. During the excitement of the fire, a number of inmates escaped, and a man was found stabbed in the heart in Colt's prison cell. The body was examined by the coroner, declared to be John C. Colt and buried within just a few short hours.

When Caroline Henshaw disappeared just a few days later, it fueled conspiracy theories that Colt had staged the whole chain of events and faked his own death, only to escape and live happily ever after. The world may never know.

In 1877, a death-row inmate named Sharkey escaped from the Tombs, poorly disguised as a woman. Two accomplices casually walked into the prison and handed Sharkey a pile of female clothing through the cell bars. Sharkey took to disguise and just as casually walked past at least two guards and out of the prison a free man. Detractors and press questioned the prison's lax security, stating, "Any decently-managed prison would have detected him before he had gone a yard from his cell."

On the early morning of August 23, 1889, four murderers were hanged together in the Tombs courtyard. Two Irishmen, one German and one black man were executed for killing women in separate incidents.

John Lewis and James Nolan shot their estranged girlfriends to death, and Patrick Packenham slit his wife's throat after a night of drinking. Ferdinand Carolin was convicted of hacking his live-in girlfriend, Bridget McQuade, to pieces after a drunken argument at the couple's apartment at 247 Stanton Street. When police first questioned Carolin, he stated that McQuade had requested to be killed. He then changed his story and said that she hacked herself to death.

On the twenty-third, the four men were woken up at 4:30 a.m., served breakfast, given their last rites and then executed two by two at about 6:49 a.m. All of the condemned remained quiet for the entire morning except for Ferdinand Carolin, who flew into fits of rage and went on long rants proclaiming his innocence.

The two Irishmen were hanged first, on the Leonard Street side of the court. As the second pair of men stood on the gallows with ropes around their necks, awaiting their turn, Ferdinand Carolin started trembling and ranting and made one final plea. "It...it...it...I'm not guilty! I didn't do this this thing!" he stuttered.

The other condemned man tuned to Carolin and said, "What do you mean? Why don't you take it like a man?"

As Carolin began to utter a reply, the trapdoor on which he was standing fell out from underneath his feet and he was executed in mid-sentence.

An 1894 *New York Times* article memorializing the old Tombs building and welcoming plans for a new structure stated, "What the

Bastille has been to France and the Newgate to England the Tombs has been to this country."

The 1902 version of Tombs prison lasted almost forty years and hosted some of the early twentieth century's highest-profile murderers, gangsters, politicians and thieves.

Yet another Tombs prison was built on this site in 1941, and the present Manhattan Detention Center, still referred to as "the Tombs," was built in 1974. The complex serves as the largest inmate receiving area in the country, houses almost one thousand prisoners and employs over five hundred corrections officers. The complex was briefly named after Mayor Giuliani's last police chief, Bernard Kerik, but Mayor Michael Bloomberg removed his name following a flood of ethical scandals that were loosed when Kerik was nominated for the position of U.S. secretary of homeland security. Kerik has already pleaded guilty to two ethics violations and is under investigation for several more.

# Mulberry Street

## *Mulberry Street at Chatham Street*

In September 1857, a group of Dead Rabbits disrupted a fire department parade procession at this intersection, causing a gunfight and small riot.

The parade was in honor of Engine Company 22, which was returning from a fire department competition in Hartford, Connecticut. Dozens of fire companies turned out for the ceremonies—complete with colored lamps, bright-colored flags, streamers and seventeen marching bands. (Believe it or not, Engine Company 22 failed to even place in the Hartford competition, but I suppose people were looking for any reason to celebrate back then.)

The problem was, many of these fire departments held professional and personal rivalries, and many were backed by separate gangs. When Engine Company 41 was passing the intersection here at Chatham and Mulberry Streets, a gang of Dead Rabbits, supporters of rival Engine Company 21 on Worth Street, attacked them with wooden clubs, brickbats and paving stones. Shots were fired, and dozens of people were involved in the mêlée, but luckily no one was killed or severely injured. Fire department chief engineer Henry H. Howard narrowly escaped being shot as a bullet passed through his hat.

This was not the case around the corner as Engine Company 41 passed the intersection of Broadway and Worth Streets and was attacked in a similar manner. However, this time two attackers, James Hanlon and James Meehan, were shot and mortally wounded.

### 7 Mulberry Street

In the mid-nineteenth century, a saloon named Mulberry Hall occupied this address and was described as a resort for "low politicians, prize-fighters, bounty-jumpers and tough men." The popular saloon was owned and operated by brothers William and Thomas "Fatty" Walsh, two of the most popular and influential Five Points politicians of the era. The Walsh brothers' story is a classic example of nineteenth-century New York City politics.

The Walsh family immigrated to New York City from County Limerick, Ireland, about 1837, when Thomas was only three years old. The family settled on Greenwich Street on the West Side, where William was born, and the brothers lived there until their early twenties. Growing up, Thomas Walsh earned the reputation of a ferocious scrapper, never backing down from a fight. As a young adult, he spent his days as a laborer, "gold-beating" at a local shop, and spent his evenings in the rowdy saloons of Five Points. It was here where he became friendly with the locals, who were drawn to his outspoken, pro-Irish nationalist views. William Walsh worked as a bookmaker, and both brothers seem to have been illiterate their entire lives.

Thomas "Fatty" Walsh became more involved with the Five Points community when he was elected to an assistant foreman

position at the local fire company. This was a huge deal during
the days when firemen were also community leaders with close
ties to gangs and politicians. For Walsh, an "Eighth Warder," to
be accepted here was quite a feat, especially in the Sixth Ward,
where outsiders were subject to extreme scrutiny. Not long after
obtaining his position as fireman, Walsh took a bullet in the leg
while covering a fellow Five Pointer in the 1857 riot with their
Bowery Boy adversaries. This demonstration of bravery and
loyalty secured Walsh's standing in Five Points and helped his
political career later on.

In early 1859, Thomas and William Walsh quit their day jobs
and opened a saloon at this address. From a business standpoint,
it was not the most desirable location. The buildings on either
side of the saloon, numbers 5 and 9, were two of the most
crowded and squalid in the city, and the rear tenement housed a
busy, converted Baptist church. But the Walshes moved here for
political reasons, as this was the heart of "Mulberry Boy" gang
territory—a group of "businessmen" that very effectively helped
mobilize the Irish vote.

The plan paid off immediately. In November 1859, William
Walsh was elected to the state assembly. Two years later, he was
elected alderman of the Sixth Ward. By 1863, he became president
of the board of aldermen and a member of the Tammany Society
general committee. Thomas Walsh followed suit and was elected
superintendent of markets in 1864.

Things were going great for the Walsh brothers for a while, until
another powerful Tammany leader, William H. "Boss" Tweed,
began controlling more and more of the organization's affairs. The
brothers did not see eye to eye with Tweed, and this caused a falling
out between the parties. The Walsh brothers were squeezed out of
the Tammany Society by the end of the Civil War. Thomas and
William went on to become outspoken critics of Tweed and leaders
of the anti-Tammany Democratic movement.

The brothers' exile from the Tammany machine was short-lived,
however. Once Tweed was sent to prison and out of the picture,

William and Thomas jumped ship again, being elected to county clerk in 1873 and assemblyman in 1881, respectively, on the Tammany ticket.

One year after being elected to state assembly, Thomas Walsh broke from the Tammany ranks once more and ran for alderman against W.P. Kirk in the 1883 election, this time for the county Democratic Party.

Thomas Walsh lost what he thought to be a crooked election and did not take it lightly. Reports say that he grew angry and threatening and was overheard saying that he was going to "do up" certain people who had opposed him. On December 20, 1883, Walsh was arrested and sent to the Tombs prison for attacking W.P. Kirk supporter Deputy Sheriff Mark Lanigan the previous day. Walsh and about fifteen friends were standing in front of the First Judicial District Court building in City Hall Park when Lanigan happened to walk by. As Lanigan passed, Walsh yelled, "There goes that big loafer now." Lanigan replied, "I don't think you can afford to call anybody a loafer," which infuriated Walsh. The two parties exchanged blows, and Walsh pulled out a knife, stabbing Lanigan in the face before bystanders intervened.

Despite the evidence and the witnesses, Walsh was not convicted. In fact, he was again elected to public office the following year and then held a job as warden of the Tombs prison between 1887 and 1889. He was fired from this position because of corruption charges.

William Walsh remained in public office through most of his life, until his death on March 7, 1878, of natural causes. He died in his home at 21 Oliver Street.

Thomas "Fatty" Walsh died in July 1899 of natural causes at his home at 48 Madison Street, which he shared with his three sisters. His daughter, Blanche Walsh, went on to become a somewhat successful actress, with two big roles on Broadway at the turn of the century. She was born at 2 Mott Street, where Thomas Walsh and his wife, a former beauty queen, first lived when they moved to Five Points.

## 11 Mulberry Street

In the mid-nineteenth century, this address served as one of the many headquarters for the notorious Dead Rabbits gang.

## 19 Mulberry Street

In the 1850s, this was the site of a saloon owned by Walter Roche, an Irish immigrant who inspired the Roche Guard political club. Legend states that there was a dispute between two factions of the Roche Guard at this location in the early 1850s that led to a rabbit corpse being thrown onto the floor during a heated argument. The Roche Guard split, and the name "Dead Rabbits" was adopted by the splinter group. More likely, the name derives from the Irish-Gaelic *dod raibeid*, in English, "tough guy."

## 27 Mulberry Street

In the mid-nineteenth century, this was another Dead Rabbits headquarters, of which the *New York Times* observed, "Scarcely a Sabbath passes during which there is not a serious disturbance of the peace, occasioned by the denizens of that locality, now tolerably well known as the 'Dead Rabbits.'"

On February 13, 1859, a small riot erupted, and several men were wounded at this location when two warring Dead Rabbits factions faced off in the street.

The trouble all started when Hugh Gillespie and a companion were walking past John Mulvihill's saloon at this address, contemplating going inside for a drink. Mulvihill himself was standing at the door and remarked that he "did not allow any such characters in his house."

A heated verbal exchange between Mulvihill and Gillespie eventually came to blows, and Gillespie ran to a neighboring saloon to seek help from Thomas "Fatty" Walsh.

Mulberry Street, circa 1910.

Walsh originally declined to help but soon changed his mind, as Gillespie was being stomped on in the street by Mulvihill. Walsh challenged Mulvihill to a fight, and Mulvihill drew a revolver, firing four shots. Walsh was hit once in the neck, at which time dozens of reinforcements from both sides poured into the streets with "pistols, knives, and clubs," and a brawl ensued.

Police from the Sixth Ward stationhouse eventually, and forcibly, quelled the fracas. Walsh survived the gunshot wound, and all of the principals involved were arrested.

## 35 Mulberry Street

In July 1885, the New York City Board of Health declared this building one of the foulest tenements in the city. The "Disinfecting Corps" was ordered to wash down this address every four weeks, along with other buildings on this section of Mulberry Street, called "the Bend," with five hundred gallons of disinfectant and deodorizing chemicals.

This mixture of chloride of mercury, chloride of potash and carbolic acid was poured and scrubbed into gutters, sidewalks, alleyways, hallways, basements and apartments, even as people slept and went on with their business.

This building was declared the worst of the bunch, where men and women were "huddled together like pigs in a pen" and

"vermin swarm in the ill-smelling rooms and cover the inmates."
One inspector even stated, "A more perfect picture of absolute
degradation of humanity could scarcely be imagined than presented
by the creatures in this apartment."

Health officers were met here by laughs and jeers from the
occupants. Some women even danced the jig and sang out loud
as the chemicals were being poured around their feet. Others
continued to sleep on benches, only to look up briefly before
"relapsing into a state of stupidity."

It took the health officers three hours to disinfect the Bend, using
fifteen hundred gallons of deodorizing liquid—that's three truckloads.

### 43 Mulberry Street

On December 4, 1892, a one-armed organ grinder named
Francisco Mele was shot and killed by 43 Mulberry Street
resident Antonio Morello. Mele was shot in the chest in broad
daylight after thirty-three-year-old laborer Morello accused Mele
of insulting his wife.

### 51 Mulberry Street

On July 7, 1859, Irish-born laborer Dennis Sullivan was nearly killed
by his wife, Margaret, in the tenement building behind this address.
Sullivan came home that night from work intoxicated and demanded
that his wife prepare him a meal. Instead, she leaped at him with a
knife and stabbed him in the neck, severing several small arteries.

### 59½ Mulberry Street

Now buried under Columbus Park, this was the address of
the notorious and deadly Bandits' Roost, the setting of the
photograph made famous by Jacob Riis in his groundbreaking
book, *How the Other Half Lives*. Riis claimed that the brick walls
of the alley and surrounding Mulberry Bend "harbored the very

A nineteenth-
century organ
grinder.

The entrance to
a rear tenement
building.

Bandits' Roost. *Photo by Jacob Riis.*

dregs of humanity" and that "every foot of it reeked with incest
and murder."

If having murderous neighbors was not enough, the Bend was
just as dangerous to one's health. In 1882 alone, diseases like
tuberculosis, measles and diphtheria claimed the lives of nineteen
young children in the two buildings that bordered the Roost, 59½
and 61 Mulberry Street.

### 88 Mulberry Street

In May 1855, Irish native Hugh Donnelly was stabbed to death in
front of this address during a dispute with a man named Gillen.
Just before the fight, Gillen was seen taking off his coat, laying it
on the ground and stating, "I can lick any Irishman on this block."
Perhaps Donnelly unwisely took the challenge.

# East Broadway

## *28 East Broadway*

In May 1903, Sadie Maltzman, a resident of this building, received a letter from a family member describing firsthand the atrocities that were being committed against Jews in the Kishineff region of Russia:

> *By the second day after Easter, about half the town was already destroyed. The mobs, seeing that they were not hindered by police, began to take lives. Jews they met in the street were struck down like dogs...Murdered people lay in the street like flies and the mobs trampled over their bodies...Some of the most prominent people in the town, government officials, and some of the great landlords took part in the massacres. Things are so bad now that the poor and destitute sometimes wish they were dead.*
> *Ida Rahatnik, Kishineff, May 3*

This gives us a good idea of why many people came to America in the first place. By 1905, local Jewish organizations had raised over $100,000 to aid victims of the Russian massacres.

## *39 East Broadway*

On June 23, 1893, Annie Victor was severely beaten in her home at this address by sewing machine company representative George Rein. Victor, who was pregnant at the time, had recently purchased a sewing machine for $5, which she was paying in installments. Rein showed up at her door demanding the full amount for the machine. When Victor produced receipts of previous payments, Rein grabbed the receipts from her hands and told her that the old salesman had "run away," so she would have to start over again. When Victor pleaded and tried to take back the receipts, Rein beat her with his fists and an umbrella. Neighbors came to her aid, and Rein was held for trail on $300 bail.

## 61 East Broadway

On September 22, 1922, On Leong Tong member Pong Tom
was found hacked to death in the hallway of this building. Pong
Tom had been struck with a hatchet over one hundred times and
strangled. Police suspected that it was retaliation for a recent Hip
Sing murder.

## 96 East Broadway

A clothing manufacturer named Herman Ostransky shot and killed
his wife and then committed suicide in an apartment here on July
25, 1917. Ostransky and his wife used to live in this apartment
with Mrs. Dora Cohen and her husband but had recently moved to
169 East Broadway because Mrs. Ostransky thought her husband
was giving too much attention to Mrs. Cohen. However, even
after moving, Herman Ostransky still visited Mrs. Cohen, which
enraged Ostransky's wife. On this day, Mrs. Ostransky followed her
husband to the apartment of Mrs. Cohen with their small child
in her arms. When she confronted her husband, he pulled out a
revolver and shot her multiple times. He then turned the gun on
himself and committed suicide.

## 153 East Broadway

In the early twentieth century, the *Warheit* was published here.
In December 1907, *Warheit* editor Louis Miller received a hand-
written death threat signed by the "Branch at Geneva of the
Union of Russia," a gang with close ties to the Reactionary Party
of Russia, nicknamed "the Black Hundred," which was supported
by the czar himself. The group accused Miller of publishing
secret Russian documents and threatened to send "three special
agents with 3,600 rubles" to kill him. There are no reports that
the group ever carried out its threats.

# The Bowery

## *22 Bowery*

On November 24, 1883, fifty-eight-year-old John Jacob Scullin was working at James and Thomas Plunket's cigar shop at this location when he became "mastered by an irresistible impulse to kill," to use his own words. At about 11:30 a.m., Scullin just walked away from his cigar-packing table, retrieved a pistol and fired on fellow employee Owen F. Plunket, who died on the spot. When police arrived, Scullin told them that he had no idea why he shot Plunket and that the two had been on good terms. He was just depressed and could not control himself.

22 Bowery today.

*Left*: 42 Bowery today.

*Below*: 46–48 Bowery today.

## 38 Bowery

This is the site of the old New England/North American Hotel, a flophouse where the "father of American music," composer Stephen Foster, lived at the time of his death in 1864.

One of the most popular songwriters of the nineteenth century, Foster penned such classics as "Oh Susanna," "Camptown Races" and "Swanee River" before losing his fortune, becoming an alcoholic and retiring to the Bowery penniless. In January 1864, thirty-seven-year-old Foster was bedridden here with a fever when he stumbled and hit his head on a washbasin next to his bed. Several hours passed before he was brought to Bellevue Hospital, where he died with thirty-eight cents in his pocket two days later, on January 13, 1864.

## 42 Bowery

This address served as the Bowery Boys' headquarters during the mid-nineteenth century. A fierce surprise raid by the Dead Rabbits on this location on July 4, 1857, sparked the infamous, bloody, two-day-long Police Riots.

## 46–48 Bowery

This is the site of Bulls Head Tavern, a Revolutionary War–era watering hole that hosted the likes of Generals George Washington (who lived at 3 Cherry Street) and George Clinton.

By 1826, this had become the site of America's first gaslit theatre, the Bowery Theatre, where the first U.S. ballet performance took place in 1827. In 1834, an angry Irish mob raided the theatre in search of English-born stage manager George Percy Farren, who many believed had made anti-American remarks. The theatre was burned down, along with several residences, but was rebuilt soon after. In the mid-twentieth century, the Bowery Theatre earned the nickname "the Slaughterhouse" for its lowbrow performances that catered to the area's growing working class. It was here where "black face" performances became popular before entering mainstream American culture.

## CANAL STREET TO DELANCEY STREET

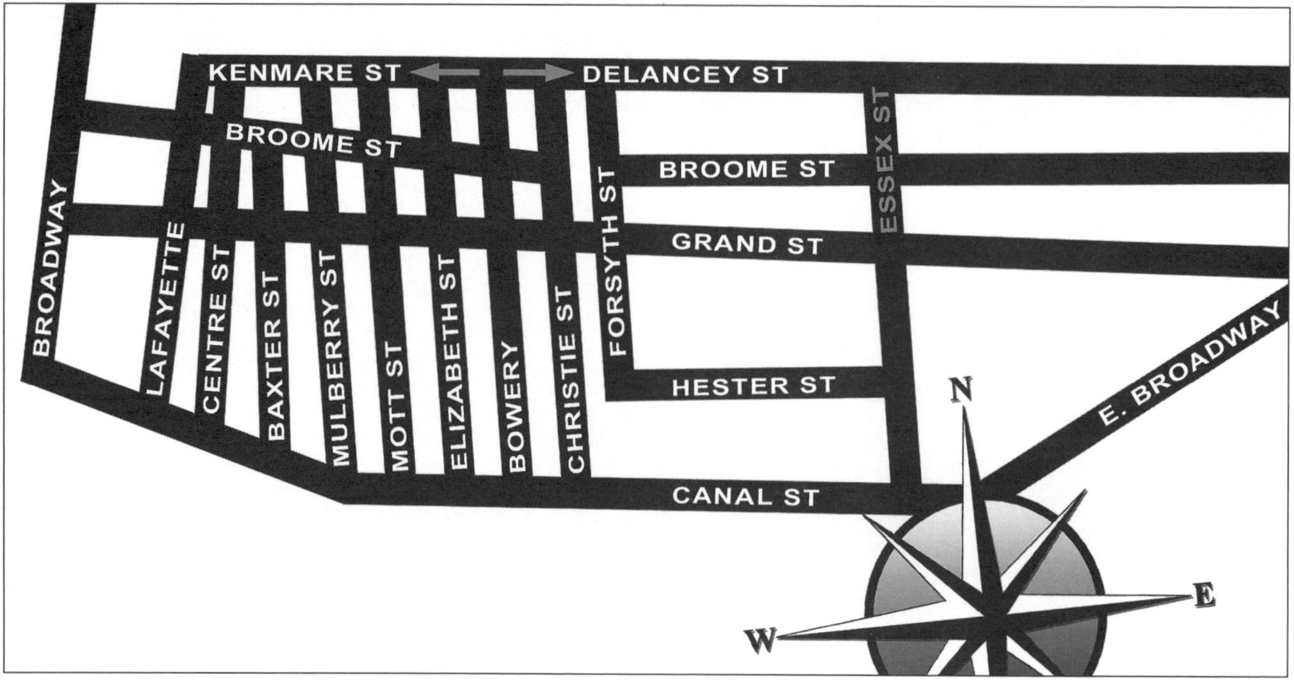

# CANAL STREET TO DELANCEY STREET

## The American Dream

Around Mulberry Street, just to the north of Canal Street, lies the neighborhood today known as Little Italy. To the immigrant Italians who settled there in the 1880s, it was not one neighborhood but several distinct enclaves—Sicilians on Elizabeth Street, Napolitani on Mulberry, Calabresi on Mott and Pugliesi on Broome. Today, the area from Canal to Delancey is mostly Chinese, as Chinatown expands to accommodate new immigrants, as well as second- and third-generation Chinese Americans who cherish their cultural ties to America's last thriving Chinatown. All that remains of Little Italy are two blocks of Mulberry and the intersection with Broome.

Unlike previous immigrant groups, the Italians maintained a close connection with their home country. It was common for Italian men to spend only a few years in the New World before returning to the Old with a bit of good American cash. Whereas the Germans, here for the long haul, built union halls and social halls to protect and promote their community, and the Irish opened Tammany Hall saloons to organize their political future, the Italians established no-interest "banks," where immigrants could store their money temporarily for the purchase of a return ticket home, one of the staple services that these "banks" offered. Banca Stabile, now the home of the Italian American Museum at the intersection of Mulberry and Grand Streets, was one of those banks.

The Italian identity of the neighborhood was anchored by the construction of specifically Italian churches when all other Catholic churches in the city were still Irish. The Church of the Most Precious Blood on Baxter Street, out of which the San Gennaro festival is organized, was the first of these. Today, the churches, cheese and pasta stores, cafés, pastry shops and restaurants are all that remain of Little Italy.

# Baxter Street

### *Corner of Canal Street*

About ten o'clock on the evening of November 11, 1857, a police officer named Carr bravely attempted to drive away a gang of Dead Rabbits from the corner of Canal and Mott Streets. Unfortunately for Carr, the Rabbits resisted and, as on many other occasions, stripped away the officer's baton and sent him on his way. Carr sought out and secured backup from both the Sixth and Fourteenth Ward police precincts and went on the hunt for the perpetrators.

They stumbled upon one of the suspects loading a pistol in a "rum hole" on one of these corners. The suspect was rushed and a struggle ensued. The Dead Rabbits responded in force, and the raiding officers were all beaten and bruised "in a most serious manner." The affray was finally quelled as a number of police officers were dispatched to the scene, but no one was arrested that evening.

### *128 Baxter Street*

On March 7, 1919, nineteen-year-old resident Lena Spinelli and her eighteen-year-old friend Josephine Gentile of 78 Mott Street were walking together on Mulberry Street near Kenmare Street when Vincenzio Papaccio opened fire on rival Giuseppi Cisere of 167 Mulberry Street. One bullet wounded the intended target, but the two young women were shot and killed accidentally. Papaccio was indicted on murder charges but fled to Naples, Italy, where the Italian government refused to honor an extradition request by President Woodrow Wilson.

## 153 Baxter Street

On November 20, 1876, twenty-three-year-old Josephine Kelly was murdered by her husband, Henry Poterson, in their third-floor apartment here. Kelly and Poterson, a young black couple, often quarreled over Poterson's jealousy. Apparently, Poterson was enraged on this particular evening after he learned that Kelly had invited a white man into their home. Poterson plunged a large pair of fabric shears so forcibly into Kelly's back that it broke through her ribs and punctured her lung, killing her within minutes. Poterson was sent to the Tombs to await trial.

## 166½ Baxter Street

In November 1888, resident Angelo Carbone went insane here at his family home after spending time in prison for the murder of Natala Brugno, of which he was falsely accused. Carbone spent four months in the Tombs and at least three months in Sing Sing prison awaiting execution before he was finally proven innocent. Even after his release, Carbone could not shake the psychological damage he endured while preparing himself for death, and he could think of nothing but impending doom even in the safety of his own home. He was declared "hopelessly insane" by a local doctor. His mother pawned all of her possessions and went broke caring for her sick son.

# Mulberry Street

## 112 Mulberry Street

In the mid-nineteenth century, this was the site of a saloon named the Little Mac Shades, owned by a gentleman called Skid Gallagher.

It is said that a desperado named "Scotty the Munger" was "shot full of holes" here by fellow patrons Tommy McAndrews and Pat McDemott during a dispute over a dogfight.

## 118 Mulberry Street

William B. Willse was killed outside a saloon here on February 13, 1879, at the hands of saloon owner Frank M'Kenna. For a reason only known to the secretive residents of Mulberry Street, Frank M'Kenna allegedly walked out of his saloon and approached Willse on the sidewalk, where he pulled out a revolver and shot Willse dead.

## 127 Mulberry Street

Casa Bella was founded in the mid-1970s by Michael Sabella, a Bonanno crime family capo. According to the testimony of FBI agent Joseph Pistone, Sabella was marked for death during a Bonanno family power struggle in the late '70s, but someone intervened and he was demoted to soldier instead of being killed.

## 129 Mulberry Street

This was the original site of Umberto's Clam House (now at 386 Broome Street), dating back to the early 1970s. The original Umberto's was owned and operated by Mathew "Matty the Horse" Ianniello, a Genovese crime family capo. Ianniello's real business was shaking down the strip clubs and porn shops of Times Square and the gay bars of Greenwich Village. From his office on the second floor, Ianniello also handled the required kickbacks from the annual San Gennaro Feast vendors on behalf of the Genovese clan. After years of FBI surveillance, Ianniello was arrested, convicted of racketeering and sent to prison.

On April 6, 1972, Columbo crime family mobster Joseph "Crazy Joe" Gallo was assassinated here at Umberto's while celebrating his forty-third birthday with his family.

Brooklyn-born Joe Gallo was a very prominent figure in the criminal world, earning the reputation as a colorful yet effective hit man. He gained the name "Crazy Joe" because of his unusually flamboyant behavior. He became friends with celebrities and socialites, was loud and told dirty jokes in front of mob wives, chewed hashish and smoked marijuana openly and dressed like a Hollywood caricature of a gangster. At Gallo's President Street headquarters in Brooklyn, he kept a live female lioness on display in a cage. All of this, along with his quick mood swings and reckless bravado, made him a curious but feared crime figure.

Joseph Gallo began his criminal career working for powerful Brooklyn mob boss Joe Profaci but grew restless and tried to overthrow Profaci in a failed bloody campaign that lasted for the better part of the late 1950s. At least a dozen mobsters were killed in what has become known as the Gallo-Profaci War. During this power struggle, Gallo forged relationships with other notable gangsters, like Carlo Gambino. In fact, it is widely believed that Gallo and his two brothers, Larry and Albert, were responsible for the murder of Albert Anastasia in 1957 on behalf of Gambino.

The Gallo brothers escaped several assassination attempts during the Gallo-Profaci War; however, Joe Gallo was arrested and convicted on charges of extortion in 1961 and was sentenced to ten years in prison. While incarcerated, Gallo made several attempts at killing fellow inmates by sheepishly inviting them into his cell and offering them homemade pasta dishes laced with strychnine. Despite the in-house murder attempts, Gallo earned an early release because he helped save a prison guard's life during an inmate riot.

Upon release from prison, Gallo essentially attempted to extort mob boss Joe Columbo for $100,000, feeling that he was owed a percentage of the family's operations from the time he was in prison. However, Columbo did not accept Gallo's demands. On June 28, 1971, Joe Columbo was approaching a podium to address the crowd of an Italian Unity Day Rally when he was shot three times in the head by an African American gunman named Jerome Johnson, who was disguised as a journalist. Columbo remained in a vegetative state for seven years before passing away, and the police suspected Joe Gallo as the brains behind the murder. No direct evidence could be found, and Gallo was not charged. However, the underworld took notice and carried the same suspicions as the police.

On the evening of April 6, 1972, Gallo threw a birthday party for himself at the Copacabana nightclub. After the party, Gallo and his family stopped into Umberto's for a late-night bite to eat. As the group was dining, the front door of the restaurant swung open and a man stepped inside, opening fire with an automatic pistol. Gallo ran for the exit but was struck three times. He collapsed on the sidewalk outside, and the gunman fled in a waiting getaway car. Ianniello was witness to the crime but claimed no responsibility or foreknowledge of the hit.

The murder of Gallo at this location was unusual for a gangland hit. It is not protocol to assassinate someone in the company of his wife and kids, but it was justified in the eyes of the mob world as retaliation for making a hit on the boss without "permission."

## 140 Mulberry Street

According to federal officials, the Gambino crime family moved their headquarters to this address after the raid of the Ravenite Social Club in 1990. It was called the Hawaiian Moonlighters Club at the time, and it is said that it was here where Peter Gotti relayed messages from his jailed brother John to the rest of the family. In 1994, the *New York Times* reported that the front door of the Hawaiian Moonlighters Club was adorned with a yellow ribbon—a Mafia symbol of remembrance for a hostage.

## 141 Mulberry Street

Café Biondo was once owned by Gambino crime family capo Joseph "Butch" Corrao, whom John Gotti referred to as "the tall kid" because of his imposing six-foot, five-inch frame. Corrao was a top man in the family and part of a tightknit Gotti crew that also included the likes of Salvatore "the Bull" Gravano and Frankie Locascio. Corrao was one of a handful of mobsters called to testify at John Gotti's 1990 trial, and a subsequent *New York Magazine* article referred to Corrao as John Gotti's "eyes and ears on the street."

## *163 Mulberry Street*

In the mid-nineteenth century, this was the home of popular fortuneteller and self-proclaimed witch Madame Leander Lent, who promised her customers "numerous wives and children." An advertisement for Madame Lent read, "Astrology. Madame Leander Lent can be consulted about love, marriage, and absent friends…at No. 169 Mulberry St., first floor, back room. Ladies 25 cents; gents 50 cents."

Madame Lent apparently ran a busy operation, which mostly catered to the naïve young Irish girls in the neighborhood, some of whom waited in line up to an hour to hear their futures. Once inside, Lent would leer into a crystal ball or cut and deal tarot cards, informing her customers of such fates as, "You will see your future within nine hours, nine days or nine weeks" and "Another woman is trying to take your man. I have something that will protect against this, but it will cost extra." The hapless victims would then be sold a potion of powder and liquid and given specific rituals to follow to protect them from their terrible fate.

On October 11, 1925, a city clerk officer named Leon Memi was found bludgeoned to death in his apartment on the first floor of this building. When police investigated the scene, they found evidence of a bloody struggle, as furniture was broken and strewn across the room and the floor was littered with broken bottles. Police also discovered jugs of whiskey and other illegal contraband associated with alcohol production, which led them to believe that this murder was the result of a bootlegging dispute.

On March 21, 1978, a New Jersey teamster leader named Salvatore "Sally Bugs" Briguglio, a suspect in the disappearance

of Jimmy Hoffa, was murdered outside of Bonita's restaurant at
this location.

### 171 Mulberry Street

This storefront once housed the Tazza di Caffe restaurant, which the
FBI believed was a Genovese crime family headquarters and social
club as early as 1981. Federal authorities bugged the restaurant in
the 1990s as part of a sting operation that targeted the San Gennaro
Feast extortion racket, which they believed was run by Genovese
capo Thomas Cestaro at this address. In 1994, a federal grand jury
accused seventy-three-year-old Cestaro of taking payments from
feast vendors, but he was never convicted or even arrested.

### 176½ Mulberry Street

The interior of this one-hundred-year-old bar has served as the
backdrop to scenes in such classics as *The Godfather III*, *Donnie
Brasco*, *The Pope of Greenwich Village* and *The Sopranos*, to name a few.
Originally named Mare Chiaro, it was recently changed to the
Mulberry Street Bar.

# Elizabeth Street

### 117 Elizabeth Street

This was once a butcher shop owned by Black Hand mob boss
Vincenzzo Cantone. In 1908, a police investigation spearheaded
by Lieutenant Petrosino led to a warrant for Cantone's arrest, but
before police could get to him, Cantone was gunned down by a
fellow gang member, perhaps to keep him from talking. It was
discovered that Cantone was suspected of nearly twenty murders
back in Italy.

# Hester Street

### *44 Hester Street*

A suicide attempt with a peculiar back story occurred here on August 25, 1885, when a man slit his own throat in the first-floor hallway during a standoff with a pair of good Samaritans. The man, named John Roggenbrod, had just assaulted a woman named Annie Deisenroth on Forsyth and Division Streets.

It all started many weeks earlier when Deisenroth disappeared from the home she shared with her husband, Andreas Eppler. After weeks of frantic searching, Eppler assumed that his wife was dead and went into mourning. A month or so later, Deisenroth reappeared. She told Eppler that Roggenbrod had kidnapped her and forced her to spend $800 in family

44 Hester Street today.

savings on him. She finally escaped when she had a chance. Eppler believed his wife's bizarre story and went looking for Roggenbrod; however, Roggenbrod found Deisenroth first, while she shopped on Forsyth Street. The two argued, and Roggenbrod beat Deisenroth with his fists. A bystander interfered, and Roggenbrod fled toward this address, pursued by men who had witnessed the assault. Cornered in the hallway, Roggenbrod pulled a knife from his vest and proceeded to cut his own throat before police could arrive.

## 165 Hester Street

On May 6, 1894, an organ grinder named Moleko was stabbed to death here during a quarrel over an Italian game of chance called "murro." The murderer, Angelo Treano, was captured a block away and sent to the Mulberry Street station for questioning.

This was also home to Jack Sirocco gang member Anthony Scantuli, known as "Tony the Cheese," in the first couple decades of the twentieth century. Scantuli was shot by members of the rival "Dopey" Fein gang on December 12, 1913, outside Madison Square Garden after an event, sparking an all-night war, with skirmishes breaking out throughout the Lower East Side.

## 189 Hester Street

On September 5, 1921, twenty-three-year-old Vincenzo Verducci, of 190 Hester Street, and three friends were riding in a cab when a man leaped from the hallway of this address, jumped on the car's running board and fired two shots at the passengers. One bullet struck Verducci in the cheek and the other smashed a bottle of champagne on the floor of the taxi. Verducci survived, and no arrests were made. The motive for the shooting was unclear.

### *204 Hester Street*

On December 11, 1921, two off-duty police brothers were visiting their mother at this address when they heard gunshots ring out in the street. The brothers, Gaetano and Vincenzo Christiano, leaped out the window onto the fire escape and found one man lying dead in the street and another man wounded. They noticed a third man running from the scene, and they gave chase, tackling him a few blocks away. The ordeal was not over, however. The brothers had to call for backup, as a crowd of up to five hundred angry and vengeful neighbors had gathered and attempted to hand out their own brand of vigilante street justice. The police had to fight the crowd with nightsticks all the way to the Elizabeth Street police station, where they learned that this was a mob revenge hit.

# Grand Street

### *183 Grand Street*

Opened in 1911, the John Jovino Gun Shop is the oldest gun store in New York City and claims to be the oldest in the United States. A 2003 Bureau of Alcohol, Tobacco and Firearms report stated that over one hundred guns traced back to this shop were used in local crimes over the previous years.

### *174 Grand Street*

This storefront has housed popular bars dating back to at least 1875, when, in February of that year, two patrons hit proprietor William Staab over the head with a fire iron after he refused to serve them alcohol.

Over the next century, the bar operated under various names like Callahan's, the Dutchman and, most notably, the Press Room, which was aptly named after it became the regular haunt

for newspaper reporters who hung out there keeping an eye on
the criminals coming and going from police headquarters just
across the street. It is said that Teddy Roosevelt was a regular
here during his tenure as New York City police chief between
1895 and 1897.

In 1909, a tunnel was dug underground from this bar to police
headquarters on Mulberry Street for easy and stealthy access
to its many services. It once hosted a gambling parlor in the
basement, a brothel upstairs and a speakeasy in the rear during
the Prohibition era. The tunnel now serves as a wine cellar for
O'Neal's bar and restaurant.

## 190 Grand Street

On May 8, 1922, two men were killed in a gangland shooting
outside of this address. A young girl, a woman and two other
innocent bystanders were also shot during the fracas. Police
believed that this was connected to the uptown assassination
earlier in the day of Vincent Terranova, younger brother of
Ciro Terranova.

Reports say that three men were standing outside of the cheese
shop at this location when two other men, the suspected targets,
turned the corner from Mulberry Street and unexpectedly came
upon the loitering group. The two men, sensing trouble, turned to
run, but the three assassins fired sixty shots from automatic pistols
into their backs. People on the street ran for cover, and the gunmen
ran off in different directions. Two detectives who heard the shots
ran after and captured one of the shooters, thirty-five-year-old
Giuseppe Masseria.

This was just one of many hits in which Masseria was involved
while climbing his way to the top of the Prohibition-era crime
world. He soon went on to control much of the bootlegging
operations in New York City and employed such criminal
heavyweights as Vito Genovese, Thomas Lucchese and "Lucky"
Luciano, who was a lieutenant in Masseria's crime family.

# Canal Street to Delancey Street: The American Dream

## *195 Grand Street*

Ferrara's is a legendary pastry shop and café that dates back to the 1890s, when it was opened by Enrico Scoppa and thirty-two-year-old Neapolitan-born Antonio "Anthony" Ferrara. This popular café is said to have been a favorite of local crime bosses like Carlo Gambino.

Ferrara's has never been directly accused of being associated with organized crime; however, a bomb that ripped apart the first floor of this café on January 20, 1929, was attributed to the raging bootlegging war of the era. Antonio Ferrara dismissed the allegations, believing that a rival baker had planted the bomb out of jealousy.

## *Corner of Grand Street/70 Allen Street*

Many people believe that this is the birthplace of Henry McCarty, aka Henry Antrim, aka William Bonney, aka "Billy the Kid."

Billy the Kid.

Sheriff Pat Garrett.

However, others dispute this claim, insisting that McCarty never stepped foot in New York City at all. There is even a question about whether his commonly accepted birth date, November 23, 1859, is accurate.

It seems that the first written account about the birth of Billy the Kid was in 1881, in Sheriff Pat Garrett and Marshall Upson's book *The Authentic Life of Billy the Kid*, which placed McCarty's birth in the "poor Irish slums" of New York City, but no one knows for sure where Garrett and Upton got their information. Many believe that Billy the Kid made up the rumor himself or that one of the writers embellished the truth a little bit. In fact, the date on which the pair claimed Billy the Kid was born also happened to be Upson's birth date.

## 350 Grand Street

The famous Seward Park High School was built on the site of the equally famous Ludlow Street Jail, a small prison that housed some of the nineteenth century's most famous criminals. In 1872, Victoria Woodhull, the first woman to run for president of the United States, was jailed here for publishing an article about an affair between Reverend Henry Ward Beecher and a parishioner of his church. In 1878, powerful Tammany Hall leader Boss Tweed died here while incarcerated, though not in a cell—he rented the warden's office.

The jail was destroyed by the turn of the century, and the Seward Park High School was built in 1929. Some of the local residents who attended the school over the years include Zero Mostel, Jerry Stiller, Walter Matthau, Bernard Schwartz (aka Tony Curtis), Julius Rosenberg and Nobel Prize–winner Julius Axelrod.

## 504 Grand Street

The apartment building at this address dates back to 1930. It was built on the site of one of the largest anti-Semitic riots in American history.

On July 28, 1902, Chief Rabbi Jacob Joseph of the United Jewish Congregation died of natural causes in his home at 263 Henry Street. It was a tremendous loss to the Jewish community because Joseph was the highest-ranking Orthodox official in the United States. Thousands of people flocked to the rabbi's home from around the country to grieve.

Two days later, on July 30, 1902, an estimated fifty thousand mourners followed the coffin of Rabbi Joseph in a procession through the streets of the Lower East Side. As the parade approached the Hoe & Company printing factory at this location, Irish factory workers jeered and hissed at the crowd. When a few leaders of the parade forced their way into the factory offices to protest, they were met with a pistol and ordered "in no doubtful language" to leave the building.

As the hearse and coffin were passing the building, a bucket of water was thrown down onto the crowd, infuriating the mourners further and prompting them to shout back. Factory workers responded by dropping bits of iron and wood and clumps of bundled paper saturated with oil down onto the shocked mourners. Some ran for cover while others stormed the factory doors and returned fire with a barrage of their own, breaking just about every window on the first two floors.

Approximately two hundred police officers were called to the scene, and dozens of rioters, including many of the mourners, were beaten back with billy clubs. During a meeting at the city marshal's office later that day, a community leader stated, "The men in the factory insulted us wantonly. Then the police, who should have protected us, clubbed us into insensibility."

In early August 1902, Mayor Low called for a complete investigation into the riot, calling the incident "discreditable to the city." Philadelphia Rabbi Bernard L. Levinthal was tapped to replace Rabbi Joseph as head of the Orthodox community in the United States.

# East Broadway

## *232 East Broadway*

This was home to "Dopey" Fein gang member Abe "Little Abie" Beckerman at the time of his involvement in the shootout at 19–21 St. Mark's Place in 1914, in which he was charged with murder. Beckerman was known as "the Forsyth Street Meal Ticket."

# Forsyth Street

## *45 Forsyth Street*

On August 2, 1880, a "very determined murder" was committed between neighbors on the first floor of this address. On the first of the month, painter and Munich native Xavier Linauer moved into the building. Three days later, mason and Prussian native Julius Frederick Munzberg moved into the apartment above Linauer with his wife and three children. Within a few days, the families began feuding, and a week before the murder, Linauer obtained a job that Munzberg also wanted, escalating the rift even further. Three days before the murder, it all came to a boiling point when one of Munzberg's sons was burned while playing with some lime in the rear court, where Xavier Linauer happened to be at the same time. When Munzberg got home, he blamed the Linauers for his son's injury and assaulted the couple, striking Mrs. Linauer in the face. Xavier Linauer then retrieved a farming trowel and beat Munzberg severely, sending him to Bellevue Hospital. When Munzberg was released, he walked into the Linauers' apartment with a heavy-caliber pistol and shot Xavier Linauer in the right shoulder. The two men wrestled, and Linauer was shot again in the kidney before he ran out the door into the street seeking help. Munzberg followed him outside and, in front of a crowd of one hundred people, shot him square in the face at point-blank range. The bullet entered Linauer's right nostril and lodged in his brain, killing him instantly.

## *107 Forsyth Street*

This was the residence of notable gang leader Benjamin "Dopey" Fein, one of the last great Jewish Lower East Side street toughs.

Like many before him, Fein was seen as sort of a local hero to many in the Jewish community. He was known to be very generous with his spoils, handing out coins to orphans and donating modest sums of money to local synagogues and community organizations. Fein's image was bolstered by the fact that he never took contracts against women—after a job in which he threw a female factory manager, who reminded him of his sister, down a flight of stairs—and he never took contracts against laborers. His marks were primarily factory managers, union leaders and company owners.

Benjamin Fein started as a young prankster on the streets after dropping out of school and slowly graduated to petty crimes like pickpocketing and robbery. Fein was known to recruit students of nearby Public School 20 to join his growing gang of thieves, promising the boys "lots of money" if they let him train them. Many youths followed, and soon Fein had a small army of pint-sized criminals to help him with his dirty work.

On October 3, 1905, Fein was arrested and locked up in the Eldridge Street Jail for robbing and assaulting two men named Robert Hoffman and Max Gordon on Grand Street. He was sentenced to three and a half years in Elmira State Penitentiary. He was locked up a couple more times in the following years, and upon his release in 1910, Fein joined up with "Big" Jack Zelig's gang and was introduced to the world of labor racketeering and strong-arm extortion. This was the beginning of the great manufacturing boom in New York City. Fein was positioning himself to corner the market on "labor-slugging."

After Zelig's death in 1912, Fein assumed leadership of his own gang, recruiting the services of such notable hit men as "Waxey" Gordon and "Little Abie" Beckerman. Though Fein is credited with almost single-handedly integrating labor unions with organized crime, many other groups challenged his monopoly, and a long war broke out between rival factions.

Fein's main rivals during this time were Chick Tricker and Jack Sirocco, two enemies of Fein's former boss, "Big" Jack Zelig. Tricker and Sirocco had gotten into the labor and racketeering game themselves; however, they took contracts from company owners and factory managers, as well as union leaders. The two gangs met for violent and deadly shootouts on numerous occasions during this time period, often when both sides showed up on the site of a labor strike.

In June 1913, Fein was accused of stabbing rival gangster "Bridgey" Webber outside of a local coffeehouse, but there was not enough evidence to convict him.

On August 10, 1913, Benjamin Fein was arrested and sent to the Tombs prison for assaulting police officer Patrick E. Sheridan at the Forsyth Street Bath House. Former lightweight boxing champ Sheridan was reportedly in the process of questioning Fein after patrons complained he was causing a disturbance when Fein attacked him. However, Fein had a different version of the event. He made a formal complaint, claiming that Officer Sheridan approached him and said he was wanted for questioning, but instead of going to the nearest stationhouse, the officer led him to Grand Street and the Bowery, where a group of police officers were waiting. He claimed that they beat him with batons and fists and put him in an ambulance, which was already at the scene, and that he had fifteen reputable witnesses to back him up. Either way, after the incident, Sheridan was promoted to detective and praised by authorities as the man who beat up the great "Dopey" Fein.

Two months later, on October 16, 1913, Fein was arrested for violation of the Sullivan Law (carrying an unlicensed pistol) and was released on $5,000 bail.

In January 1914, Benjamin Fein and his gang ambushed a contingent of the Sirocco gang during a party at Arlington Hall on St. Mark's Place. County clerk officer Frederick Strauss was the only casualty in the ensuing gun battle, and Fein was arrested, along with a handful of associates, for the murder. He made a deal with authorities—his freedom in exchange for information on the gang and associated union activities.

Fein was set free and, to say the least, lost a lot of friends. He fell out of the spotlight for a while until July 1931, when he was arrested, along with Samuel Hirsch and Samuel Rubin, for throwing acid on local businessman Mortimer Kahn. Ten years later, in 1941, Fein and fellow small-time gangsters Herman Fogel, Abraham Cohen, John Ferraro and Samuel Klein were arrested during a raid for possessing $10,000 worth of stolen garments. During the trial, Fein was accused of stealing more than $250,000 worth of clothing and fabric over a three-year period. He was considered for a sentence of life in prison but was spared and sent to Sing Sing for his final prison stay. After his release, Fein settled down and became a tailor, a trade his father had taught him as a youth. He raised a family in Brooklyn and died of natural causes in 1962.

After Benjamin "Dopey" Fein's arrest in 1914, the gang's rates were published in the *New York Times*. The price for raiding a small manufacturing plant was $150; larger factory shake-ups would cost more, up to $600. The price for "shooting a man in leg or clipping his ear off" was only $60 to $90, depending on the importance of the target. For something very specific, like hiring out the gang "for the purposes of throwing an objectionable manager or foreman down an elevator shaft," the fee was $200. And the ultimate "knockout" (a murder) was $200 as well.

## 121 Forsyth Street

On January 14, 1877, a sixty-one-year-old German immigrant named Frederick Krick was killed in the rear tenement building of this address. In the late hours of this particular night, Krick, depressed and out of work, set out to shoot his wife and twenty-year-old son, firing three shots at them that just missed. His son, George Krick, grabbed an axe and struck his father several times on the head until he fell unconscious. George ran away but turned himself in a short time later; his story was corroborated by his mother, and he was not convicted.

# Broome Street

## 385 Broome Street

In the 1970s, Café Roma was run by feared Genovese crime family underboss Carmine "Little Eli" Zeccardi. According to informant testimony, Zeccardi was actually acting boss of the family from 1972 to 1974 but was passed over for Frank Tieri when it came time to elect an official leader. From then on, the informant testified, Zeccardi felt betrayed and his relationship with the family deteriorated. New boss Tieri allegedly felt that Zeccardi was a threat to his throne and possibly believed a coup attempt was imminent. In 1977, Zeccardi disappeared in what is still an unsolved mystery.

### 396 Broome Street

In the early twentieth century, Little Rock's Poolroom at this location served as headquarters to Chick Tricker and Jack Sirocco, two of the most notable gangsters of the era.

Tricker was a longtime Eastman gang member who teamed up with Sirocco after the latter jumped ship from the Five Points gang. The pair eventually started a war with "Big" Jack Zelig to assume control of the Eastman gang when leader Max "Kid Twist" Zwerbach was killed in a Coney Island dispute with Five Pointer Louis "the Lump" Pioggi.

In one incident in the summer of 1912, "Big" Jack Zelig drew a weapon on Chick Tricker in this building's hallway. Zelig pressed the gun to Tricker's stomach and declared that he was going to kill him. Tricker responded by saying, "Go on. You wouldn't shoot anybody who was looking at you. Beat it now before I do you up." Sensing

Max "Kid Twist" Zwerbach.

Louis "the Lump" Pioggi.

that Zelig was second guessing his actions, Tricker continued, "Why you mutt, you haven't got the nerve to touch a soul."

Zelig chickened out and slowly backed away until he made it to the street, where he ran to Jimmy's Mandarin Café on Doyers Street to rally his troops. Several Zelig gunmen geared up and ran toward Tricker's saloon but were met by a large and heavily armed contingent of Tricker supporters. Zelig's men ran for their lives without a shot being fired.

Little is known about Chick Tricker's early life, but he first gained attention in the criminal world by insulting a dancer at the Five Points gang headquarters, the New Brighton Social Club on Great Jones Street. Five Points gang member, former prizefighter and notorious bouncer at McGurks Suicide Hall, "Eat 'Em Up" Jack McManus took offense to Tricker's comment, and the two got into a confrontation outside the club. Tricker was shot in the leg during the dispute. The next day, while Tricker was in the hospital recovering from his wounds, Jack McManus was knocked unconscious with a newspaper-wrapped metal pipe by a Tricker associate.

Later on, Chick Tricker teamed up with former Five Points gang member Jack Sirocco in a failed attempt to overthrow "Big" Jack Zelig by leaving Zelig behind to take the rap during a bank robbery in 1911. Zelig was injured and arrested, but Tricker and Sirocco refused to bail him out, assuming that they could take unified control of the Eastman gang in his absence. Jack Zelig had very powerful connections at Tammany Hall, however, so the charge did not stick—Zelig was released within days, sparking a war between the factions.

# The Bowery

## *101 Bowery*

In 1840, after traveling with a circus company in the Mississippi area, P.T. Barnum arrived back in New York City to find new opportunities. One of his very first business ventures was a "shoe-blackening, cologne and bear's grease" store at this location, but it ended up being short-lived, as his partner, a man named Proler, fled the country with "all the property he could lay his hands on." Barnum left the failed business and became manager of the Vauxhall Gardens Saloon later that year, before going on to open the American Museum of Living Curiosities downtown and, of course, "the greatest show on earth," which we know today as the Ringling Bros. and Barnum & Bailey Circus.

In the late twentieth century, this was coincidently home to another museum of living curiosities, owned by E.M. Worth. Worth's museum boasted some of the most sensational displays of its day, including one of the finest specimens of Architeuthis—giant squid—in North America. The twenty-eight-foot-long squid was captured off the coast of Newfoundland in 1881, shipped to New York City on ice and purchased by Worth, who preserved the creature in alcohol.

On July 7, 1882, Worth was bitten by one of the fifty-four live rattlesnakes that were kept in a display case of the museum.

P.T. Barnum.

Worth routinely fed the snakes raw meat after hours, which almost
proved fatal on this occasion as the bite sent him to the hospital in
a "comatose condition." Worth survived the ordeal and earned the
dubious distinction of being the first person treated for a rattlesnake
bite in New York City history.

## *103–105 Bowery*

This was the address of a notorious late nineteenth-century saloon
owned by popular local Owen Geoghegan. "Owney," as he was
known, was born in Ireland about 1837 and immigrated to New York
City at the age of ten. As a young man, he earned the reputation of
a courageous pugilist fighting for cash in underground contests on
the docks along the East River. Entering professional, bare-knuckle
prizefighting, Owney bested some of the era's greatest boxers. Not
the most technical of fighters, Owney relied on brute force and often
used dirty tactics to win matches. In the fifth round of a match against

101 Bowery today.

fellow Irishman Con Orem, Owney claimed that his opponent was wearing brass knuckles. When Orem dropped his defense to show the referee that he was clean, Owney knocked him out.

Owney Geoghegan used his earnings and connections to open a "sporting house" on Twenty-third Street and First Avenue, where he posted a standing challenge to box any man who dared step in the ring with him. Owney won time after time, and the legend of his power grew—until it was discovered that he concealed a pair of heavy iron horseshoes in his gloves.

This sports club became the headquarters of the murderous Gashouse gang, with which Owney developed a close relationship. So close was the relationship that when Owney was sentenced to Blackwell's Island prison for assaulting a patron of his club, the Gashouse gang attacked the prison transport truck and freed Owney, who went into hiding for a year. He never served his sentence.

In 1880, Owney Geoghegan opened this nightclub at 103–105 Bowery, where it quickly earned the reputation as being one of the roughest establishments in the city. Fights, shootings, stabbings and police raids were regular occurrences. Owney himself killed a local street tough named Johnny Rose inside the club but was never charged. The club racked up over one hundred indictments, but Owney's political connections kept him in business—until 1883, when he was busted for regularly allowing boys as young as ten years old to frequent the bar. Owney was sentenced to Blackwell's Island prison, where his health declined and he became mentally unstable. Upon his release, Owney retired and moved to San Francisco, where a bank that held all of his savings went bust, and he lost all of his money.

Owney Geoghegan died soon after, broke and destitute, of natural causes in "Patsy" Hogan's sports club in Hot Springs, Arkansas. He was forty-eight years old.

### 114 Bowery

This was a saloon owned by the legendary Steve Brodie, who, in July 1886, claimed to have jumped off the Brooklyn Bridge and

103–105 Bowery today.

survived. The rumor inspired a Looney Tunes cartoon called
*Bowery Bugs* and a Hollywood movie starring George Raft called *The
Bowery* and coined a popular turn-of-the century phrase, "pulling
a Brodie."

Steve Brodie, a professional gambler and race walker from the
Lower East Side, made his way into pop culture consciousness by
supposedly attempting this stunt on a dare, just months after daredevil
Robert Odlum was killed while attempting the same thing.

As Brodie began publicly planning his jump, a liquor dealer
named Moritz Herzber offered to finance a saloon for Brodie if he
was successful. After the jump (which nobody actually witnessed),
Herzber made good on his promise, and this saloon, which also
served as a museum dedicated to the stunt, was opened.

114 Bowery today.

The public could not get enough of Steve Brodie, who went on to tour the country in the vaudeville musicals *Mad Money* and *On the Bowery*, in which he recreated his famous leap for fans.

Eventually, Brodie settled in Buffalo, where he died from diabetes in 1901 at the age of thirty-eight.

## *164 Bowery*

In June 1917, Giuseppe "the Boss" Masseria was arrested for trying to shake down Simpson's Pawn Shop, which was located at this address. Masseria was sentenced to four years in Sing Sing prison for this crime.

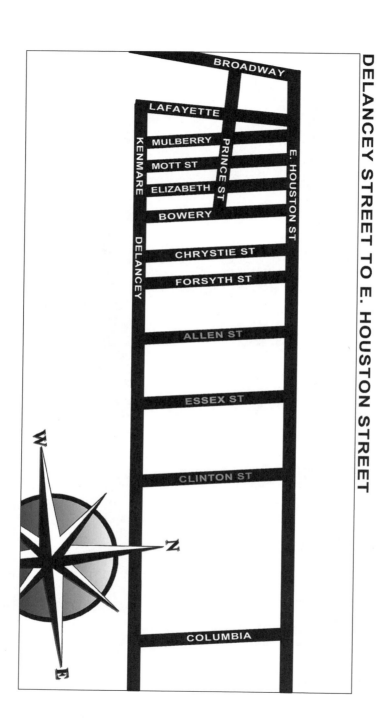

DELANCEY STREET TO E. HOUSTON STREET

# DELANCEY STREET TO EAST HOUSTON STREET

## The Promised Land

North of Delancey is still historic Little Italy, but Chinatown has not yet expanded into it. This neighborhood has succumbed to a different expansion—the spread of gentrification from nearby SoHo. In keeping with the trend in syllabic acronyms, the area has been dubbed by the real estate industry "Nolita": North of Little Italy.

It was once a far cry from gentrification, the heart of Prohibition bootlegging and Mafia racketeering. The Italian immigrants' close ties to southern Italy and Sicily extended to the extortionist societies of both regions. The Neapolitan Camorro, Sicilian La Cosa Nostra and the Black Hand were not neighborhood gangs so much as hermetic gangster rings that preyed on their own people. Economic abuse of Italians by Italians pervaded the character of their slum existence. The padrone lorded over the Italian children with Dickensian brutality, dictating their labor and collecting their earnings. The Black Hand had no compunction about attempting to extort from even the most famous national heroes: Enrico Caruso, the greatest living opera singer of his day, a symbol of Italian pride, received the paper notes stamped with a black-ink hand demanding $15,000, a fortune at the turn of the century. Whether this model of internal violence reflected a fear of outside authority, alienation from their new home or merely the convenience of the nearest and most familiar target,

the gangsters of the Prohibition era seem to have preserved it
in their motto, "We kill only each other," which prevented the
mob from rubbing out its non-Italian political enemies. The worst
violence of the Mafia has always been reserved for Italians, often
for its own members.

# Delancey Street

### *25 Delancey Street*

In 1914, this was the address of notable gangster Irving Wexler,
alias Harry Gordon, alias "Waxey" Gordon, during his time as
gunman for "Dopey" Fein's gang. (Wexler had also previously lived
at 102 Eldridge Street.)

Wexler was born about 1886 on the Lower East Side to working-
class Jewish immigrant parents, and like many criminals of the
era, he took up the craft of pickpocketing at an early age. By the
first decade of the twentieth century, Wexler had grown close to
neighborhood thug Benny Fein, and the pair became very successful
as guns-for-hire during labor disputes.

"Waxey" Gordon.

## Delancey Street to East Houston Street:
## The Promised Land

On November 28, 1913, Wexler was arrested at the scene of a strike break at Max Feldman's hat factory, located at 166 Greene Street. Three people were injured during a shootout as Fein's gang was sent to protect the workers who were threatened with violence after walking out on the job just days earlier.

On January 15, 1914, twenty-eight-year-old Wexler was arrested but soon released for his part in the murder of Frederick Strauss at Arlington Hall, during the infamous shootout between the Fein and Sirocco gangs.

On July 18, 1915, Wexler was arrested while swimming in a public pool uptown by the man who famously beat up Benny Fein, Detective Patrick Sheridan. The detective actually dove into the pool to make the arrest after identifying Wexler, swimming underwater and emerging beside him saying, "Hi Waxey!" Wexler was wanted for the February 20, 1915 robbery of a wholesale business at 383 Grand Street.

By 1919, Wexler had become friendly with the likes of "Lucky" Luciano, Meyer Lansky and the great Arnold Rothstein, whom Wexler convinced to invest $175,000 in a bootlegging operation that transported alcohol across the Canadian border and into cities throughout the East Coast and Midwest. The business worked out so well that by the early 1920s, Wexler had become one of the most powerful bootleggers in America, earning an estimated $2 million a year.

Wexler's power began to decline after the death of Rothstein in 1928. His relationships with Luciano and Lansky also deteriorated as the factions fought over the direction of the business at the end of Prohibition. Luciano and Lansky felt that Wexler had to be removed from the picture, so they supplied federal authorities with information on Wexler's tax practices.

On May 21, 1933, acting on a tip provided by Luciano and Lansky, police raided Wexler's Catskills hideout, and he was arrested for evading almost half a million dollars in taxes. Wexler was sentenced to ten years in prison. Upon his release from jail, Wexler moved to California, where he used his old connections to start a successful drug-smuggling operation. In 1951, sixty-two-year-old Wexler was arrested for trying to sell heroin to an undercover police officer and was sentenced to twenty-five years in Alcatraz, where he died of natural causes on June 24, 1952.

# Mott Street

## *210–214 Mott Street*

This address housed an extravagant mercantile goods store, owned by prominent Italian mobster Ignazio Saietta, aka Ignazio "the Wolf" Lupo, at the turn of the century. Sicilian-born Saietta is often credited as the father of the Italian Mafia in America and is suspected of being responsible for close to sixty murders.

In 1910, Lupo and fellow Mafia boss Giuseppe Morello were indicted on counterfeiting charges. They received lengthy thirty- and twenty-five-year sentences, respectively. Saietta was released early for good behavior in 1920, and after about two years in Sicily he returned to the United States and attempted to regain power—but the underworld in 1922 was a much different place than it had been a decade earlier. Prohibition was in full swing and the powers that be had little room for another boss. Saietta was forced to stay out of bootlegging and was relegated to organizing small extortion, gambling and lottery rackets in Brooklyn.

He was sent back to prison one final time in 1936 on extortion charges. By the time he was released, Lupo was old and frail, having spent the better part of his life behind bars. He died of natural causes in 1947 and is buried at Calvary Cemetery in Brooklyn, alongside his family and a red-carpet list of criminals and Mafia icons.

# Mulberry Street

### *Intersection of Mulberry and Kenmare Streets*

During Prohibition, this was known as "Curb Exchange," an open-air, underground market of sorts where alcohol was distributed by bootleggers after being imported from distilleries in places like upstate New York and Pennsylvania.

In the 1920s and '30s, a restaurant named Celano's Garden was located on this corner at 36 Kenmare Street. The owner was good friends with Lucky Luciano, and it was here that Luciano set up shop while working for Giuseppe "the Boss" Masseria. It was a strategic location. Luciano's job was to keep an eye on the alcohol trade of Curb Exchange, with the help of future Mafia stars Vito Genovese, Thomas Lucchese and Frank Costello. Masseria met with Luciano at Celano's often to discuss business, but dining with Masseria was not a pleasant experience. Joseph Bonanno compared Masseria's eating habits to those of a "drooling mastiff." Luciano was reportedly repulsed by Masseria—he spit food when he spoke and let food dribble down his chin onto his shirt. He would eat large meals two-fisted and with verve. Masseria was the epitome of gluttony, where Luciano considered himself to be sophisticated and reserved.

The FBI accused Luciano of running his business out of Celano's as late as 1936, when he was indicted on running a $12 million a year prostitution ring, selling narcotics, tax evasion and perjury and was sentenced to thirty to fifty years in prison.

### *217 Mulberry Street*

In March 1908, a fifty-five-year-old Italian immigrant and former Franciscan monk named Vincenzo Bonanno was found mutilated and bludgeoned to death in a Twenty-ninth Street building. Bonanno, a resident of a boardinghouse at this address, was lured to his death by two mysterious people for unknown reasons. He was not robbed—all of his jewelry was still intact—but someone had beaten the man with a hammer, as well as sliced his eyes and nearly decapitated him with a straight razor. Both the hammer and the razor were found in the room where the murder took place, along with the only other evidence police had to go on—a handkerchief with the initials "C.G." that one of the murderers had left behind. Police believed that this murder was the result of a religious feud that originated back in Sicily, where Bonanno was a monk of the Franciscan order. A fellow Franciscan monk named Father Leo had been murdered while preaching at his altar in Denver, Colorado, just a month earlier.

## 236 Mulberry Street

This was the site of the Latone & Guidetti funeral parlor, where on August 13, 1912, hundreds of neighbors passed by to pay their final respects to five neighbors who were electrocuted at Sing Sing prison. The five men, of Italian descent, were convicted of the attempted robbery and murder of Mrs. Mary Hall near Croton Lake, in Westchester County, the previous year and put to death on August 12. Many in the Italian community felt that the group's conviction and execution were ethnically biased and that the men were targeted because they were Italian immigrants.

## 247 Mulberry Street

This fortified brick building is most famous for being John Gotti's headquarters, the Ravenite Club, in the 1970s and '80s, but it has served as a meeting place for some of the most notable gangsters in American history dating back to the 1920s and '30s, including "Lucky" Luciano.

John Gotti's rise to power started early when he was a young street tough running with local small-time gangs on the streets of Brooklyn after dropping out of school in the eighth grade. By his twenties, Gotti had become well known in the underworld for his particular talent

John Gotti.

at making money hijacking freight trucks at nearby JFK airport. The Gambino crime family took notice, and Gotti formed a relationship with a well-respected underboss named Aneillo Dellacroce, whose headquarters were here at 247 Mulberry Street.

In 1968, at age twenty-eight, John Gotti spent his first stint in prison on hijacking charges. It was here where he befriended the Bonnano crime family by confronting fellow inmate Carmine Galante. Galante was the "warden" of the Mafia population at the prison, and Gotti, though not yet officially a "made" man, stepped up to Galante and requested a share of the gangster's prison spoils for himself and the other connected men who were incarcerated. Galante, it is said, was so impressed with Gotti's boldness that he asked him to join the Bonnano family. Gotti refused, as his allegiance was with the Gambinos.

Upon release from prison, Gotti went right back to work for Dellacroce, who saw a lot of potential in young Gotti and appointed him chief of his own crew in Queens. In 1973, John Gotti was tapped to carry out his first assassination on behalf of the Gambino family. A man named James McBratney was fingered as the ringleader of a crew who kidnapped and murdered Carlo Gambino's nephew. On May 22, 1973, Gotti and Angelo Ruggiero walked into a bar on Staten Island disguised as police officers and gunned down McBratney, killing him on the scene. Both Gotti and Ruggiero were arrested and convicted of the crime, but with the help of Gambino family attorneys, they were only sentenced to a maximum of four years in prison.

Carlo Gambino died in 1976 while Gotti was still in prison. There was a huge shake-up in the underworld because Gambino left the throne to his brother-in-law and cousin, Paul Castellano, whom many felt did not deserve the position. Castellano did not rise through the ranks like the rest of the family. He was involved in the business end of operations but was not a tested soldier like the man many believed should have been in power, underboss Aniello Dellacroce. A power struggle was brewing, and John Gotti was about to step right in the middle of it.

John Gotti was paroled in 1977 and sworn in as a full-fledged member of the Gambino crime family in a ceremony presided over by Paul Castellano. Gotti, like many other family members, did not quite see eye to eye with his new boss. Castellano was known for being a very distant and hands-off boss, opting to spend much of his time in his mansion on Staten Island instead of fraternizing with other family members. Many felt that he lost touch with the streets and the codes of the underworld.

On February 25, 1985, Paul Castellano and Aniello Dellacroce, along with the bosses of the other four New York Mafia families, were arrested and indicted on charges of extortion, racketeering and murder as part of the famous Mafia Commission Trial. While out on bail, rumors circulated (no doubt encouraged by John Gotti) that Castellano was going to strike a deal with the FBI and rat out the rest of the crew for a reduced sentence.

On December 16, 1985, two weeks after Dellacroce died of lung cancer, Castellano was gunned down outside of a Midtown restaurant on the orders of John Gotti. It was this incident that made Gotti the new boss of the Gambino crime family. He continued to run his operation out of this building, along with notable associates like Salvatore "Sammy the Bull" Gravano, Angelo Ruggiero and Frank LoCascio.

On December 11, 1990, local and federal authorities raided the Ravenite Social Club and arrested John Gotti, along with Gravano, LoCascio and Thomas Gambino. Gravano reportedly felt that Gotti was going to let him take the fall, so he made a preemptive deal to testify against the family. Gravano's testimony, along with FBI surveillance tapes recorded here at the Ravenite, helped convict Gotti and LoCascio to life sentences without the possibility of parole. Gravano was sentenced to twenty years.

John Gotti died of natural causes behind bars in 2002. His brother, Peter Gotti, took over as head of the family until his arrest in 2003 for his alleged part in the attempted extortion of movie star Steven Seagal and plotting to kill Salvatore Gravano, among other charges.

The Ravenite building was seized by the government in 1998, ending an eighty-year history of criminal enterprises. It now houses a retail designer store.

# Elizabeth Street

## *164 and 166 Elizabeth Street*

On February 25, 1907, a bomb went off that resulted in the destruction of the first floors of these buildings and the shattering of surrounding tenement windows. Two police officers just missed "being blown to bits" as they ran to stomp out the sparks that were discharging from a suspicious box in front of the building. The bomb was intended for Michael Angelo Alonge, proprietor of a grocery store who refused to pay a $600 Black Hand extortion fee. His business was ruined.

## *226 Elizabeth Street*

This address was home to Sicilian-born Giuseppe Morello, one of the most powerful mob bosses in America at the turn of the century. Early on, Morello teamed up with another local mob boss, Ignazio "The Wolf" Saietta, and began a campaign of terror and influence that lasted more than two decades. The team specialized in counterfeiting but increasingly relied on Black Hand extortion tactics, using extreme violence and intimidation to achieve great success. Police believe that the infamous 1903 barrel murder of Benedetto Madonia took place in the basement of this building, before the encased body was dumped at East Eleventh Street and Avenue D.

Within the first decade of the twentieth century, Morello's gang, which included his two brothers, Antonio and Niccolo, and two half brothers, Vincenzo and Ciro Terranova, had expanded its power beyond New York City. It organized criminal enterprises in Chicago, New Orleans, Pittsburgh, Philadelphia and other American cities while keeping close ties to the Mafia in Sicily. Morello and Saietta set up headquarters at 8 Prince Street and began enterprising rackets in counterfeiting and real estate. One of their properties was a horse stable at East 108th Street and 1st Avenue that became known as a "murder factory." As many as sixty people were murdered at these stables over two decades. Many victims were reportedly hung on meat hooks or burned alive in furnaces.

Morello and Saietta were finally sentenced to lengthy prison terms in 1909, as part of a U.S. Secret Service sting operation. While incarcerated, Morello and Saietta lost most of their power to rising stars like Giuseppe "the Boss" Masseria and Salvatore "Toto" D'Aquila, with whom Morello ended up going to war after his release from prison in 1920.

On August 15, 1930, Giuseppe Morello was gunned down at his office on 116th Street, along with two associates, Joseph Perrano and Gaspar Pollaro.

## Delancey Street to East Houston Street: The Promised Land

### 240 Elizabeth Street

On January 24, 1908, a bank located at this address was blown out by a bomb after proprietors Pasquale Pati & Sons refused to pay a Black Hand demand. This was just one of dozens of Black Hand–related bombings to take place in the city over a two- to three-year period.

# Forsyth Street

### 217 Forsyth Street

This was home to a young Giuseppe "the Boss" Masseria for about three years upon his arrival in New York from Sicily in 1903. Masseria would rise through the ranks of the criminal world to become the leading Prohibition-era bootlegger and boss to such notable crime figures as Joe Adonis, Thomas Lucchese, Vito Genovese and Charles "Lucky" Luciano.

# Prince Street

In the first couple decades of the twentieth century, the stretch of Prince Street between Bowery and Elizabeth Streets was referred to as "Black Hand Block." On January 7, 1911, police raided the block, entering several establishments and arresting thirty-four people believed to be involved in organized crime.

### Broadway and Prince Street

In June 1840, a large log cabin was erected at this intersection to advertise presidential candidate William Harrison. Harrison won the election and became the ninth president of the United States but died only thirty-one days later after catching a cold, presumably during his lengthy inaugural address.

# A History and Guide to Gangsters, Murders and Wierdos of New York City's Lower East Side

On January 23, 1989, FBI agents arrested John Gotti, Angelo Ruggiero and Anthony "Tony Lee" Guerrieri on this corner, just one block from the Ravenite Social Club. They were charged with the attempted assassination of John F. O'Connor, the vice-president of Local 608 of the United Brotherhood of Carpenters and Joiners.

## 8 Prince Street

At the turn of the century, this was the headquarters of powerful mob bosses Ignazio "the Wolf" Saietta and Giuseppe Morello, two of the most successful and violent gangsters of the era. Both Saietta and Morello were Sicilian immigrants who fled to New York to avoid murder charges and became related when Saietta married Morello's half sister, Salvatrice Terranova. At this location, the pair ran a saloon in the front and a restaurant in the back. Their venture into counterfeiting began at this address, where crude reproductions of two- and five-dollar bills were shipped to the restaurant from Salerno hidden in containers of olive oil, spaghetti, cheese, wine and other food products. They sold the fake bills to wholesalers throughout the country at thirty to forty cents on the dollar, which prompted the attention of the U.S. Secret Service. The restaurant was raided, and the pair was arrested several times, but charges did not stick until 1909, when both men were sentenced to long prison terms, diminishing their power on the streets.

Morello ended up being assassinated in 1930 after a brief return to power, and Saietta died of natural causes in 1947, less than a month after being released from a second lengthy stay in federal prison.

## 23 Prince Street

In the 1960s, this was home to the Thompson Social Club, an organized crime hangout operated by one-time "Lucky" Luciano and Vito Genovese enforcer Joseph "Joe Beck" DiPalermo. A 1964 Senate report listed DiPalermo as a key figure in a multimillion-dollar heroin ring based out of Miami.

## Northwest Corner of Prince and Lafayette Streets

Fifth president of the United States James Monroe died on this site on July 4, 1831. The Federal-style town house that once sat on this corner was owned by former president Monroe's daughter, Maria, and her husband, Samuel L. Gouverneur, the first couple to be married in the White House.

Monroe moved in with his daughter after the death of his wife, Elizabeth, in 1830. He died a short time later of natural causes and was originally buried at the Gouverneur family's vault in the New York City Marble Cemetery on East Second Street. His body was moved in 1858 to the Presidents Circle at the Hollywood Cemetery in Richmond, Virginia.

## 27 Prince Street

This Ray's Pizza is the original "Famous Ray's," dating back to 1959. Original owner Ralph Cuomo opened the shop in the front room of his family home at this address. He called it Ray's instead of Ralph's because his nickname was Ray, an abbreviated version of his Italian given name, Raffaele.

Cuomo was sent to prison in 1971 for his part in a heroin racket, which he ran out of the basement here on behalf of the Lucchese crime family. This sweeping federal sting netted fifty-four people in four U.S. cities on charges of conspiring to sell, transport and conceal $25 million worth of heroin. Cuomo was sentenced to four years in federal prison.

The building's mob ties did not end there, however. In 1978, four members of an organized crime crew that had set up headquarters here were arrested on charges of bribing a probation official.

Fifty years before Ray's Pizza opened its doors, on December 20, 1909, a bomb ripped through the first floor of this five-story tenement house, leaving a two-foot-wide hole in the floor. The bomb was left at the door of a man named Domenico Ambrose, who lived here with his wife and four children. Police believed that this was retaliation from a Black Hand crew that was sent to jail for kidnapping Ambrose's niece four years earlier. The family had been receiving threats from friends of the convicted kidnappers.

# Columbia Street

### 6 Columbia Street

This is the site of the boyhood home of Meyer Lansky, architect of the twentieth-century American Mafia. Lansky is one of the most well-known and influential organized crime figures in American history. (Please note that this building no longer exists.)

Born Majer Suchowliński on July 4, 1902, Lansky was raised at this address after his family immigrated to New York City from modern-day Belarus in 1911. Lansky was a quiet and intelligent yet feisty and curious young boy. He attended local public schools, where he befriended a neighborhood thug named Salvatore Luciana ("Lucky" Luciano's birth name). Lansky was one of the few who stood up to young Luciano's bullying, and the two grew to respect each other.

As a boy, Lansky learned the trades of tool and die making and auto repair and worked in a factory and as a mechanic for a short time before he decided to put his talents toward more lucrative endeavors. He teamed up with neighbor Benjamin "Bugsy" Siegel and began an auto theft racket. Siegel would steal the cars and Lansky would "fix them up" and resell them.

There is an odd story about how Lansky and Siegel actually met. It is said that on October 18, 1918, Lansky was walking home from his job when he heard the screams of a girl coming from a nearby building. He supposedly picked up a crowbar and entered the building to investigate. Inside, he found Charles Luciano attacking Benjamin Siegel. Lansky reportedly hit Luciano over the head with the crowbar to prevent the assault on a fellow Jew, at which time police arrived, arresting everyone. According to legend, Luciano caught Siegel sleeping with his girlfriend and went crazy, assaulting both Siegel and the girl, and Lansky walked in on the middle of it.

Another, less far-fetched story is that Lansky befriended Siegel after he witnessed him in a street fight during a craps game that went wrong. Lansky was impressed by Siegel's toughness and recruited him on the spot.

Whatever the circumstances, the pair became good friends and more deeply involved in criminal activities around New York City, eventually forming the "Bugs and Meyer mob," a tightknit crew of guns-for-hire that included Joseph "Doc" Stacher, Joe Adonis, Abner "Longie" Zwillmen and Arthur "Dutch Schultz" Flegenheimer. It was about this time that criminal heavyweights such as Arnold Rothstein and the Five Points gang took notice, recruiting the Bugs and Meyer mob for several strong-arm jobs.

In 1931, after the murders of Giuseppe Masseria and Salvatore Maranzano, Meyer Lansky was appointed to a leadership position in Lucky Luciano's new National Crime Syndicate organization. Here, he orchestrated the Mafia's decades-long influence on labor unions, shipping and trucking companies, public works projects and, of course, gambling in America.

By 1932, Lansky and partner Frank Costello were setting up slot-machine franchises and gambling casinos in Mafia-friendly cities around the country. These franchises were being funded by a finely organized drug-smuggling operation.

In 1941, Meyer Lansky created the Nevada Projects Corporation and sent Benjamin Siegel out to Las Vegas to invest in the area's up-and-coming gambling industry. Within a few short years, the mob had infiltrated the Las Vegas strip and controlled many of the casinos and resorts in the city.

During World War II, Lansky was so powerful that he was allegedly approached by the United States government to enlist his aid in securing a top-level domestic security weakness, New York Harbor. Assistant District Attorney Murray J. Gurfein introduced high-ranking naval officers to Lansky's attorney, former U.S. attorney Moses Polakoff, who in turn introduced them to Lansky. The government was looking for help securing the Mafia-controlled shipping yards along the Hudson and East Rivers, which were being infiltrated by Nazi U-boats. In order to accept an offer, Lansky said that he had to consult with his boss, Lucky Luciano, who was doing time in federal prison for tax evasion and running a multimillion-dollar prostitution racket. Shortly after the first meeting, in May 1942, Luciano was moved to a more convenient location—Great Meadows prison outside of Albany, New York. During this time, he was visited on several occasions, not only by Lansky, but by several naval officers as well.

Lansky ended up making a deal that set Luciano free from prison, and in exchange, Lansky had his associates turn over shipping-related union books, provide secretive surveillance information on local ports and supply security along the waterfront.

However, many accounts of this story claim that it was actually the other way around, insisting that it was Lansky and company who extorted the U.S. government into freeing Lucky Luciano. They supposedly set off a bomb on a ship being built in the harbor to "entice" the government into making a deal.

Either way, key Mafia figures in America got a free ride for a while for their assistance, giving Lansky and Luciano the opportunity to expand their gambling empire by setting up casinos in New York, New Jersey, Arkansas, Louisiana, Florida, Nevada and even Cuba, in a deal with Cuban leader Fulgencio Batista that lasted until Fidel Castro's overthrow in 1959.

Meyer Lansky was at the peak of his career in post–World War II America. He is credited for pioneering the use of offshore banking to launder U.S. dollars around this time and is said to have made deals with the CIA to traffic large amounts of heroin from the Far East for distribution in the United States.

Finally, in 1972, Lansky and associates were indicted on federal tax evasion charges. Lansky skipped bail and sought refuge in Israel; however, when Prime Minister Golda Meir learned about Lansky's mob connections, she had him deported from the country.

Lansky was denied entry into many other countries until he finally returned to the United States to face charges, which he ended up beating. Retiring to a Miami condo, Meyer Lansky died of natural causes on January 15, 1983, claiming that he earned only $22,000 a year.

### *46 Columbia Street*

Notorious Jewish mobster Benjamin "Bugsy" Siegel was raised at this address, after his family moved here from his birthplace across the river in Brownsville, Brooklyn. (Please note that this building no longer exists.)

Benjamin Siegelbaum was born on February 28, 1906, to working-class parents who had recently immigrated to the United States from modern-day Ukraine. After dropping out of school in the eighth grade, fifteen-year-old Siegel joined forces with the more mature nineteen-year-old Meyer Lansky, forming a criminal enterprise that would span several decades.

In 1926, at the age of twenty, Benjamin Siegel was arrested for allegedly raping a neighborhood girl, who some believe was working for Siegel as a prostitute. However, it is said that the woman was persuaded to change her story and the charges were dropped.

Bugsy Siegel's work as a strong arm and hit man for hire with the Bugs and Meyer mob gained him the attention of prominent criminals like Arnold Rothstein. Along with Lansky, Siegel rose through the ranks of the Prohibition-era crime world by being a dedicated and efficient soldier in the bootlegging wars.

On April 15, 1931, Siegel, along with Vito Genovese, Albert

Benjamin
"Bugsy" Siegel.

Anastasia and Joe Adonis, was hired to murder Joe "the Boss"
Masseria in a Coney Island restaurant in a hit orchestrated by
Lucky Luciano.

In December 1931, Benjamin "Bugsy" Siegel was charged, along
with five other gangsters, including Harry Greenberg and Louis
Kravitz, under the new "public enemy" law, alleging that the men
were involved in racketeering and extortion. Two gangsters were
indicted while Siegel used his connections to go free.

On November 9, 1932, Bugsy Siegel survived a hit attempt
by a rival Italian gangster while attending a meeting with other
top mobsters at the Hard Tack Social Club on Grand Avenue in
Brooklyn. The assassin lowered a bomb through the chimney of
the roof but failed to realize that the shaft was offset by a right

angle, so the bomb got stuck between floors before it exploded. The blast sent debris flying across the table at which the gang was sitting and injured several people, but no one was killed. Siegel received a two-inch scar on his forehead from a piece of flying brick, which he bore his entire life. The would-be assassin was tracked down and murdered within two weeks.

In 1937, Lansky sent Benjamin Siegel to California on a mission to convince West Coast criminals to work with the Syndicate. By the 1940s, New York and Chicago mobsters had taken control of California's gambling and racing rackets, all spearheaded by Meyer Lansky. The "new" American Mafia even got involved with the motion picture industry in Hollywood, to which Siegel was instantly drawn. He would become friends with movie producers, actors and agents and date Hollywood starlets while doing screen tests and getting head shots for himself. Siegel's good looks and powerful connections opened a lot of doors for him in California, which worked to the advantage of the Mafia—for a while.

Siegel actually had the chance to alter world history in 1938, when he was invited to a party thrown by his mistress, Italian countess Dorothy Taylor Di Frasso, at the opulent Villa Madama in the foothills of Rome, Italy. Some unexpected guests showed up— Hermann Goering and Joseph Geobbels, two high-ranking officials of the German Nazi party who were old friends of the countess and in town for a weapons demonstration. This infuriated Siegel, who threatened to kill the men right there on the spot, but Countess Di Frasso talked him out of it, claiming that revenge would be taken out on her family.

In the summer of 1946, Siegel began construction on the Flamingo Casino and Resort in Las Vegas. There were already a handful of casinos popping up farther down the strip, but Siegel envisioned a lavish palace resort for A-list celebrities and wealthy businessmen farther north, in a location that many believed was inconvenient and doomed from the start. Siegel quickly ran out of his own money due to a series of mishaps and scams, so he secured enough capital to finish the project from old friends Meyer Lansky and Lucky Luciano, among others. By this time, the FBI had begun to compile what would become a twenty-four-hundred-page file on Bugsy Siegel.

Benjamin Siegel was reportedly charming but naïve; he did not possess the same intellect or business skills that made Lansky and Luciano so powerful. He ended up being ripped off by shady contractors, who often charged Siegel twice the value of materials needed to build the Flamingo. His arrogance led him to take charge of the design concept of the resort, even though he had no training as an architect. This led to several redesigns and renovations that ran the budget over $6 million, double the original estimate. In the end, this mismanagement, along with his growing ambitions in Hollywood, which many felt were jeopardizing the Mafia's financial interests, led to Benjamin Siegel's murder.

On June 20, 1947, while Siegel was sitting on the couch reading a newspaper in his mistress actress Virginia Hill's mansion in the Hollywood hills, an unknown gunman shot him multiple times through the window, killing him instantly.

To this day, Benjamin "Bugsy" Siegel's murderer is unknown, though several experts trace the hit back to Lucky Luciano and lifelong friend Meyer Lansky.

# The Bowery

## *207 Bowery*

This is the address of the late nineteenth-century Comanche Club, headquarters of Tammany Hall boss Big Tim Sullivan. It was one of four saloons that Sullivan owned in the area and the location of his wake, where hundreds of people gathered after his death in 1913.

## Delancey Street to East Houston Street: The Promised Land

### *241 Bowery*

This building once hosted a saloon owned by Chick Tricker, longtime Eastman gang member and eventual leader in the gang's final years.

On June 4, 1912, Tricker was standing in front of his saloon when three taxicabs drove by and shot at him. Tricker survived the assassination attempt by ducking into the building.

### *257 Bowery*

On March 25, 1889, John Keenan was working at a mustard factory at this address when his coat got caught in a revolving belt, dragging him through the machine over forty times before it could be shut down. Keenan miraculously survived with a broken arm, internal injuries and various cuts and bruises.

### *288 Bowery at East Houston Street*

In 1858, this was home to Empire Hall, a rowdy saloon with a terrible reputation in the community. The proprietor was a Dead Rabbits gang member named Thomas Ryan, who lived at 20 Mulberry Street.

On March 24, 1858, a squad of detectives from the office of the deputy superintendent raided Empire Hall, and thirty-five patrons were arrested while trying to scale a wall in the rear courtyard. As gang members and associates were being led off, a row of gratified neighbors cheered and howled. All thirty-five men and women were sentenced to prison for various lewd activities.

# E. HOUSTON STREET TO E. 14TH STREET

EAST RIVER PARK

FDR DRIVE

AVE D

SZOLD ST

AVE C

AVE B

TOMPKINS SQUARE PARK

AVE A

1st AVE

2nd AVE

3rd AVE

4th AVE

E. HOUSTON ST

STUYVESANT

ST. MARKS PL

E.7th ST

E.6th ST

E.5th ST

E.4th ST

E.3rd ST

E.2nd ST

E.1st ST

COOPER SQUARE

BOWERY

GREAT JONES

BOND ST

BLEECKER ST

E.13th ST

E.12th ST

E.11th ST

E.10th ST

E.9th ST

E.8th ST

ASTOR PL

LAFAYETTE

BROADWAY

# EAST HOUSTON STREET TO EAST FOURTEENTH STREET

## A Radical New Direction

Following the anarchist assassination of Czar Alexander, blamed on Jews, pogroms spread through Russia and the Ukraine, spurring a mass exodus. New York became their safe harbor and last hope. But poverty in close quarters breeds gangs and crime, and the Jews were no exception. At the turn of the century, half the prisoners in Sing Sing were Jews.

The Jewish and Italian gangs in the East Village clashed not over politics but over illegal rackets. The earlier battle between American-born and immigrant labor gave way to turf battles between two equally recent arrivals. They fought over every enterprise available to them, perhaps the biggest and most available of which was the unions, with their sisters, brothers, fathers and mothers all members. Gangsters infiltrated the unions, turning the already violent labor movement into a criminal racket, replete with gang warfare. By the time Prohibition rolled in, the scene was set for rampant murder.

Despite the pervasive presence of criminality in the slums, the ghetto was far from a depressed neighborhood. The most densely populated two square miles on the face of the earth, it was overflowing with culture and politics. At a time when New York was still a colonial backwater, its elites deeply conservative, the slums were a hotbed of the avant-garde, the recent immigrant arrivals from Europe bringing new European ideas and new European culture. It was a world center of anarchism, with the great Johan Most and Justus Schwab and their protégé, Emma Goldman, speaking and demonstrating in the streets and in the union halls, writing and plotting in their apartments and prison cells.

Culture was irrepressible. Yiddish theatre, Lincoln Steffens pronounced, surpassed Broadway. All the radical new plays of Europe were eagerly mounted in Yiddish. Oscar Wilde's Salomé, too risqué for conservative Protestant Broadway, became Bessie Tomaschevsky's signature role. The first American school of painting, the Ashcan School, found a home in the free anarchist "Modern School," with George Bellows and Edward Hopper's teacher, Robert Henri, on the faculty and Man Ray and John Sloan attending as students.

In 1921, the federal government imposed quotas on European immigration. With no new immigrant arrivals, and the second generation looking for any avenue out, the slums emptied quickly. Rents plummeted. Only marginals and artists found the neighborhood still attractive. St. Mark's Place in particular, with its proximity to long-haired, intellectual Greenwich Village, became a mecca to the Beat Generation, jazz musicians, abstract expressionists and countercultural activists of every stripe. Eventually the hippies arrived, the Yippies and Weathermen, and off off Broadway radical theatre, experimental theatre and transvestite theatre; later, squatters, punk rockers and "crusties" came, along with the Puerto Rican immigration that gave us the poetry slam, graffiti art and the urban mural.

# East Houston Street

## *Northeast Corner of East Houston and Bowery*

According to garden associates, mob heavyweight Vincent "the Chin" Gigante harvested tomatoes here at the Liz Christy Gardens in the 1980s.

# East Houston Street to East Fourteenth Street:
## A Radical New Direcation

### *46–48 East Houston Street*

At the turn of the century, this was home to the laboratories of iconic scientist and inventor Nikola Tesla. Born in the Austro-Hungarian region of Croatia in 1856, Tesla fled his war-torn country for New York City at the age of twenty-eight with reportedly only four cents in his pocket. Tesla soon found a job with another contemporary icon, Thomas Edison, but they had a falling out over money and ideals. Tesla was forced to find work as a laborer to support himself and his projects, which included the world's first AC induction motor in 1887. The AC motor won him acclaim and landed him a contract with Westinghouse, thus beginning the famous "war of the currents" between Tesla's AC electric project and Edison's DC electric project.

Tesla opened his lab at this location in 1891, the same year he became an American citizen, and performed extraordinary experiments—pioneering everything from early robotics and radio transmitting to "electrical healing."

In some cases, Tesla's experiments got a little out of hand. One day, soon after opening his laboratory, Tesla was testing the effects of extra low frequency waves on structures of various sizes when he decided to attach a hand-sized, low frequency vibrator to a steel beam of the building. Within a few minutes, the windows of surrounding buildings began to shatter and the earth began to shake, sending residents fleeing and seeking shelter. Police arrived at the lab within a few minutes to find Tesla franticly swinging a sledgehammer at the device, trying to dislodge it from its post. When the device was deactivated, the shaking stopped, but not before the building suffered structural damage. Tesla would not reveal to police what caused the small earthquake, but in an interview later on he described a similar device called a "telegeodynamic oscillator," which, he said, "is so powerful that I could now go over to the Empire State Building and reduce it to a tangled mass of wreckage in a very short time" with a device you can "slip in your pocket."

### *146 East Houston Street*

This was home to Max Green, a strikebreaker who was shot to
death by members of the "Dopey" Fein gang during a labor dispute
on November 28, 1914.

# Mulberry Street

### *300 Mulberry Street*

This was the site of New York City police headquarters until
1909. Teddy Roosevelt was stationed here as police commissioner
between 1895 and 1897.

# Lafayette Street

### *375 Lafayette Street*

On February 26, 1922, a sightseeing bus full of tourists was passing
this address when passengers witnessed the murder of Joseph Marone,
a petty thief who had crossed a local gang and was executed in broad
daylight. If there can be anything funny about this, it would be the
fact that the tourists initially thought they were witnessing the filming
of a motion picture. I imagine it did not take long before excitement
turned to terror when they realized there were no cameras.

It seems that 196 Mott Street resident Joseph Marone was a
marked man; he was wanted for lying to a gang about his share
of a burglary, which was strictly against the criminal code of
ethics. Marone apparently knew that he was marked because he
left his house only during the day and walked only on the busiest
of thoroughfares, hoping to discourage any murder attempts. The
bustling midday foot traffic did not deter the brazen killers, however,
and Marone died without giving any clues about his assailants.

# The Bowery

## *295 Bowery*

On this northeast corner of Bowery and East First Street stood undoubtedly the rowdiest and most notorious turn-of-the-century saloon in all of New York City, McGurk's "Suicide Hall." The legendary roughness of McGurk's made its way into pop culture and inspired a number of early twentieth-century songs, plays and works of literature.

Irish immigrant John McGurk opened his saloon here in 1895 after operating several other small dives in the area. It quickly became a favorite haunt for seedy businessmen, corrupt politicos, petty thieves, gamblers, pickpockets, prostitutes, gang members, panhandlers and sailors alike. It is said that McGurk's business cards made their way to every seaport in the world, attracting tens of thousands of daring men and women a year to the saloon, where they were entertained by piano players, small bands, singing waiters and "professional" women who worked the crowd. The waiters would carry "knockout drops," small doses of liquid camphor, which they mixed into unsuspecting patrons' drinks before dragging them out back into Horseshoe Alley and robbing them. The alley, now the luxury apartment building's main entrance on First Street, was said to be pitch black even in the middle of the day. The crowd was tough, but the staff was tougher. Just about everyone employed by John McGurk possessed a criminal record, and the saloon boasted the most formidable bouncers since Monk Eastman.

McGurk's earned the name "Suicide Hall" as it became the venue of choice for the downtrodden to end their lives. Dozens of suicide attempts occurred at the saloon; a half dozen were successful in 1899 alone.

In January 1899, a saloon waiter named Charles Steele robbed and killed a man during a home invasion on Seventh Street. After the crime, Steele sought sanctuary inside McGurk's, where police tracked him down and arrested him.

On March 10, 1899, John McGurk was arrested for "keeping and maintaining a disorderly house." He was released on $500 bail.

In March 1900, McGurk's was raided. Manager George Furman was arrested and held on $1,500 bail. Later that month, John McGurk's nephew, Philip "Strauss" McKenzie, and a bartender at the saloon were arrested for following an intoxicated patron outside and then assaulting and robbing him on the corner of Bowery and Bleecker Street. McKenzie was sentenced to Elmira Reformatory, and the bartender was given ten years in Sing Sing. By the way, McKenzie had only one eye—the other one was lost in a fight with bouncer "Eat 'Em Up Jack" McManus.

By the beginning of 1901, local police began cracking down on the Lower East Side's vice district, closing down and patrolling brothels and "questionable" saloons. McGurk's was closed but reopened under a new name within days, with a new sign that did not bear the name of John McGurk. A barker stood out front assuring all comers that "the old place is still McGurk's and has not moved away."

A raid on the "new" McGurk's in March 1901 netted the arrests of several people, including manager George Kennedy of 303 Bowery.

In February 1902, employee Bart O'Connor was arrested during a raid on McGurk's but escaped under police custody. John McGurk fled the city with his family to escape prosecution and settled in California, where he died of natural causes in 1913 at the age of fifty-nine.

## 323 Bowery

An unnamed clerk working at a drugstore at this address was one of 152 victims to die on August 12, 1896, during a blistering summer heat wave. Another 68 New Yorkers were overcome by the heat on the following day, bringing a five-day total to 362 victims.

## 373 Bowery

In the mid-nineteenth century, this was home to Madame Prewster, the "Pioneer Witch of New York." Madame Prewster is considered by many to be the first fortuneteller in the city and was called "the most dangerous of all" in the 1850s due to her unscrupulous and illicit operations.

In an advertisement for her services, Madame Prewster claimed that Napoleon was a regular client.

# Broadway

## *818 Broadway*

In the 1880s, this building served as John Morrissey's popular 818 Broadway casino. It was called the "best-known gambling joint in the country." The casino's service, décor and fairness were "exceeded by nothing this side of the Atlantic."

One of the many great politicians bred by Tammany Hall, John Morrissey (born February 12, 1831, died May 1, 1878) was an Irish immigrant, street brawler, Dead Rabbits gang leader, bare-knuckle heavyweight champion, casino owner and eventual state senator (1866 and 1868) and U.S. congressman (1875 and 1877). Morrissey was an undefeated professional prizefighter who once took the American championship title belt away from "Yankee" Sullivan in a contest that lasted thirty-seven rounds.

Morrissey earned the nickname "Old Smoke" early in his career, after a fight in a saloon. He was pinned to a coal stove by his adversary when a sudden burst of energy propelled Morrissey to finish the fight—with his jacket still burning from the stove.

Morrissey's arch rival as leader of the infamous Dead Rabbits was Bowery Boy William "the Butcher" Poole (born July 24, 1821, died March 8, 1855). As tough as Morrissey was, Poole was equally as ferocious. The two met for a bare-knuckle street fight in 1854. Poole reportedly was the victor when Morrissey called "enough" only five minutes into the fight. Both men were scarred for life after that brawl.

The *New York Times*, reporting on Morrissey's condition after the fight, stated, "His eyes were closed and one of them was found to be gouged from one end of the socket...There is a hole in his cheek, and his lips are chewed up in a frightful manner."

Morrissey and pal Lew Baker went on to shoot and kill Poole in a bar fight on Broadway a year later. Poole's final words were reportedly, "Today I die a true American."

### Broadway and East Eleventh Street, Southwest Corner

In the mid- to late nineteenth century, the ritzy Saint Denis Hotel stood on this corner. One of the hotel's most notable guests was the wife of assassinated president Abraham Lincoln, Mary Todd Lincoln, in September 1867.

Mrs. Lincoln registered under the name "Mrs. Clark" and was accompanied by her servant, a former slave named Lizzie Keckley. The pair came to New York to sell clothing and jewelry in an attempt to raise some much-needed money.

The plan did not go well, and the two left New York City within a few days, after being swindled by hucksters. Soon after, a series of high-profile embarrassments landed Mary Todd Lincoln in a mental institution for four months.

The Saint Denis Hotel was also the site of the world's first public demonstration of the telephone. On May 11, 1877, Alexander Graham Bell made a call to his assistant in Brooklyn from the second floor's "gentleman's parlor" in front of a thrilled crowd of two hundred invited guests.

# Second Avenue

### 19 Second Avenue

On the lot of this northwest corner of East First Street now sits a new luxury apartment building. The Italianate tenement-style building it replaced housed the restaurant on the first floor that John and Joe Wheiler reportedly used as headquarters for their drug and racketeering operation during the first couple decades of the twentieth century. The two brothers, known as Johnny and Joey Spanish, were rivals of gangster Nathan "Kid Dropper" Caplin (better known as Kaplan) .

On July 29, 1919, Nathan Kaplan assassinated Johnny Spanish on this corner, ending once and for all a rivalry that terrorized the Lower East Side and claimed many casualties.

Johnny Spanish, a ruthless figure with a terrifying reputation, was referred to by a 1911 *New York Times* article as the "Successor of Monk Eastman." He controlled a very powerful and violent gang and was said to have been ready to use any of the four revolvers, brass knuckles or blackjacks that he carried with him at the drop of a dime on any hapless victim. He had a notorious temper and was known to unleash his terror on a bet or a dare from a friend.

Nathan Kaplan was no lightweight either. He was a reputable street tough who started his career as con man, thief and extortionist at a very early age. Kaplan's skills eventually caught the eye of the Five Points gang, which he was a member of until at least 1911.

Kaplan got his nickname "Kid Dropper" from a street scam he perfected called "the drop." There are many variations of this scam, but the basic concept is as follows: A con man inconspicuously drops a wallet full of fake cash, and when a passerby goes to reach for the wallet, he reaches at the same time. The con man then says that he is in a rush but will offer the passerby the wallet to claim for reward in exchange for a certain amount of money. The con man takes off with his bounty, and the victim is left with a fake wallet. (Apparently, this scam still exists. A man on my walking tour recently told me that he fell for the same trick in Times Square, only this time it was a roll of "silver dollars.")

Kaplan once worked for the Johnny Spanish gang, but the pair never really got along. They always fought over business and women, but kept it somewhat civil for the greater benefit of the business. However, taking advantage of a lengthy prison term Spanish was serving for the murder of an innocent girl during a shootout, Kaplan gained control of much of the operations. He became one of the most powerful post–World War I crime bosses in the city.

When Spanish was released years later, the two gangsters fought a bloody war over control of the labor-slugging racket before Kaplan finally put an end to the feud. Spanish was meeting his wife at the restaurant here when Kaplan and at least one accomplice walked up to him and shot him multiple times in the chest. Spanish died a couple days later at Bellevue Hospital.

Nathan Kaplan's business thrived for a while after the murder of his main rival, but competition was increasing. It is reported that up to 60 percent of all clothing worn in America was manufactured in New York City during this era, so there was a lot of opportunity for criminal influence and battle for control of various operations was fierce. By the 1920s, heavyweight gangsters like Jacob "Little Augie" Oren, Louis "Lepke" Buchalter and "Gurrah" Shapiro muscled their way into the labor-slugging business, and Nathan Kaplan's empire was being challenged.

On August 28, 1923, Kaplan was placed into the backseat of a police car in front of the Essex Street Courthouse (now the Essex Street market) after being arrested for carrying a concealed weapon, when a gunman sent by Jacob Oren opened fire on the defenseless Kaplan, killing him in front of a crowd of witnesses.

Oren took over Kaplan's operations until he was killed in 1927, presumably at the hands of Louis Buchalter.

## 32–34 Second Avenue

Originally, this lot housed a five-story tenement building that hosted a restaurant on the first floor in the early twentieth century.

On March 5, 1912, Antonio Campioni of 117 Essex Street was leaving the restaurant with a companion, sixteen-year-old Nicola Sorentino of 208 Thomson Street, when at least five shots were fired by a man waiting outside the door. Campioni was shot once in the mouth and once in the back of the head. He later died of his wounds at Bellevue Hospital.

# East Houston Street to East Fourteenth Street:
## A Radical New Direcation

In the summer of 1913, ten architects were chosen by the city to submit plans for a new Second Avenue Courthouse, intended to help relieve the burden of the other three municipal buildings in the area—the Essex Street Court on Essex Street, the Second Municipal Court on Madison Street and the New York County Jail on Ludlow Street.

In 1979, Jonas Mekas and his Anthology Film Archives bought the Second Avenue Courthouse building from the city for $50,000. They spent $1.7 million to renovate the building. The courtrooms were made into sixty-six- and two-hundred-seat auditoriums; the jail cells became offices and storage space.

## *76 Second Avenue*

In the late nineteenth century, this building was home to a large German beer hall owned by J.W. Guentzer. On October 27, 1884, an attack that started over a political argument left three men, patrons Charles Bernhart and Phillip Straub, and the proprietor's son, Michael Guentzer, in near-critical condition.

A man named Thomas Kraupa and his friend Peter Kehr got into a quarrel with Bernhart and Straub inside the saloon. According to records, Kehr lost his temper, struck his antagonist with a cane and was quickly ejected from the bar, along with Kraupa. It seemed that the trouble was over, until a short time later, when Phillip Straub exited the bar to head to his home on East Fourth Street. Kraupa was waiting outside, and when Straub stepped through the door, Kraupa slashed Straub's face with a large knife.

When Bernhart and Guentzer responded to Straub's cry for help, they were stabbed and slashed multiple times in the head, face, arms and torso. Luckily, all parties survived the ordeal, and Straub was convicted of attempted murder.

By 1894, the first floor of 76 Second Avenue was home to the Tilden Club, a meeting hall for local political organizations, and the upper floors were used as a boardinghouse. On June 16,

1894, boarder John Renard committed suicide here by drinking strychnine. He was despondent over falling into poverty after months of unemployment.

In April 1895, former New York assemblyman Otto Kempner gave a speech here at the Tilden Club on the "career and collapse of the New York State democracy."

By the first couple decades of the twentieth century, this was the address of Segal's Café, a notorious Jewish mob hangout that was a haven for street thugs, con men and organized criminals alike. Segal's Café was owned and operated by Louis "Little Louie" Segal and Aaron "Big Aleck" Horlig.

In June 1912, the crew at Segal's Café set off bombs at three locations around New York City, targeting businesses associated with rival gambling parlors.

Bombs went off within fifteen minutes of one another. The first was the Unique Cigar Store at 85 Fourth Avenue—a police officer and two women were injured. The second target was 103 Fourth Avenue, home to Stoloff & Co. Supply Store. No injuries were reported, but the storefront was blown out. The final target was the Central Café and Vienna Restaurant, at 6 St. Mark's Place. Again, no injuries were reported, but severe damage was done to the first few floors of the building.

According to the *New York Times*, police raided Segal's Café and arrested "Big" Jack Zelig, who told police lieutenant Charles Becker, "It's a good thing you saw me first, for I would have filled you full of lead."

This confrontation was most likely a ruse on the public because it was Becker himself who hired Zelig and his gang to make extortion collections on his behalf. Becker, an ex-Bowery bouncer, was a personal friend of Zelig's old boss, Monk Eastman. Eastman introduced Becker to "Big" Tim Sullivan, who in turn helped Becker enter the police force and rise through the ranks.

Jack Zelig (born Zelig Harry Lefkowitz on May 13, 1888) started his criminal career at nine years old, quickly earning a reputation as a skilled pickpocket. By age thirteen, he was known

"Big" Jack Zelig.

as one of the best thieves in New York City, under the tutelage of the Crazy Butch gang.

By the time he was seventeen years old, Zelig was a full-fledged member of the powerful Eastman gang, serving as lieutenant to Max "Kid Twist" Zwerbach. After Zwerbach's murder at the hands of the Five Points gang in 1908, Zelig assumed control of many Eastman gang members.

Zelig was a notorious street and knife fighter, dubbed "the most feared man in New York" by local authorities, and had his hands in just about every kind of criminal activity on the Lower East Side. The gang used murder and intimidation to terrorize rivals and the public alike. Members robbed the brothels, casinos and banks that were not already under their control; they extorted local business owners and smaller gangs; and they even provided their expert services to those who could afford to pay for it.

A former Zelig gang member turned police informant handed over the following menu of the gang's services: a slash on cheek with a blade was $1 to $10; a shot in the leg or arm was $5 to $25; throwing a bomb was $5 to $25; and a murder was only $10 to $100.

Some notable associates of Zelig's included "Waxey " Gordon, Harry "Gyp the Blood" Horowitz, Jacob "Whitey Lewis" Seidenshner, Louis "Lefty Louie" Rosenberg and Francesco "Dago Frank" Cirofisi.

Harry Horowitz started out as a petty thief and bouncer at some of the roughest saloons on the Lower East Side. He became known as the "best bouncer since Monk Eastman," which was no small feat. He was a tall and incredibly strong individual who was said to pick up grown men and break their spines over his knee.

Horowitz muscled his way to the top of the Lennox Avenue gang, which he led in his final years. The Lennox Avenue gang became a satellite gang to Zelig's and provided extra muscle when needed.

Jacob Seidenshner was a known bruiser and powerful pugilist. Under the tutelage of Jack Zelig, Seidenshner became one of the gang's most accurate and efficient hit men.

Louis Rosenberg was a petty thief and hired gun. He never shied away from pulling a trigger, but he was not a coldblooded killer like some of his colleagues, such as Fransesco Cirofisi, who only took jobs that guaranteed bloodshed.

## *80 Second Avenue*

This building was home to Giuseppe "Joe the Boss" Masseria, bootlegging kingpin and arguably the top boss of the New York Mafia in the 1920s. Masseria recruited some of the most important Italian criminals of the twentieth century, like Vito Genovese, Frank Costello and Thomas Lucchese. In fact, Lucky Luciano was Joe Masseria's lieutenant and right-hand man. Countless times, Luciano would pull his car up to this curb, smoke a cigarette and wait for his boss at the door. He would escort Masseria to the car, open the door for him and drive off for business.

Sicilian-born Masseria was known in the crime world as a "Mustache Pete"—the term for a very conservative, old-school gangster clinging to old-world ideals. Masseria forbid doing business with anyone who was not full-blooded Sicilian and believed in the traditional rituals of initiation into the family. Many of the younger Americanized gangsters like Lucky Luciano only really cared about making money, not century-old rituals. After all, this was a new century, a new era. There were new technologies and new opportunities. Luciano was already associating with the likes of Meyer Lansky and Bugsy Siegel behind Masseria's back.

The Castellamarese War, the infamous "bootlegging war," broke out at the height of Prohibition when Salvatore Maranzano organized against Giuseppe Masseria to reorganize the Mafia under his control in a move that was sanctioned by the Mafia back in Sicily. Dozens of mobsters were targeted, and both sides suffered heavy casualties during this war. Maranzano ended up convincing Luciano and crew to turn on their boss and work for him. They may have had no choice—Maranzano was winning the war, and they were guaranteed to be future targets.

On April 15, 1931, Luciano picked up Masseria and drove him to an Italian restaurant in Coney Island for dinner. During an after-dinner game of pinochle (an Italian card game), Luciano excused himself to the restroom and in rushed Vito Genovese, Albert Anastasia, Joe Adonis and Bugsy Siegel, who shot

Frank Costello.

Masseria to death at the table. He died on the floor, clutching an ace of spades.

Now Luciano and crew worked for Sal Maranzano—until they realized that Maranzano was even more strict than Masseria and shot and stabbed him to death in his office in Midtown.

This is a very important time in the history of the American Mafia. Luciano took over and, with the help of Meyer Lansky and others, organized the Mafia Commission and took control of the newly formed Five Families of the Italian Mafia. The families still exist and are known today as the Bonanno, Gambino, Genovese, Columbo and Lucchese crime families. Luciano's plan was to eliminate the rituals, concentrate on making money nationally and discourage tyranny. There was no more "boss of bosses"; there were now five families that shared resources and settled disputes politically for the greater good of making money. Luciano, Vito Genovese, Thomas Lucchese and Frank Costello all went on to became heads of families.

## 82 Second Avenue

On August 9, 1922, Joe "the Boss" Masseria walked out of his apartment at 80 Second Avenue and was rushed by two men who began firing at him. Masseria ducked into a store here at 82 Second Avenue with the gunmen in pursuit. Once inside, Masseria fired back, hitting one of the assassins. With weapons empty and the store in shambles, the gunmen fled across Second Avenue to a waiting getaway car, which was idling just around the corner on East Fifth Street. The men jumped on the running boards of the Hudson Cruiser, retrieved new weapons and sped west on East Fifth Street toward the Bowery, guns blazing.

Unfortunately, they didn't get very far. Call it bad timing, bad luck or both, a garment industry union meeting had just ended and dozens of laborers were milling around in the street. When they heard the shots and saw the speeding Cruiser coming down the street, they tried to stop it. The gunmen plowed through the

Also Roadster type. Also Cabriolet completely enclosed, quickly changeable to open Roadster

**HUDSON MOTOR CAR COMPANY,** 7808 JEFFERSON AVENUE, DETROIT, MICHIGAN

A Hudson Cruiser.

crowd and shot randomly at the blockade, hitting six and killing two (plus a horse).

When police arrived on the scene at 82 Second Avenue, they found Joe Masseria in his upstairs bedroom at 80 Second Avenue, shell-shocked. He was sitting up in his bed, dazed, and his ears were ringing from the proximity of the weapon fire. Incredibly, he was unscathed—except for two bullet holes through his straw hat, which he was still wearing on his head.

The gunmen were Umberto "Rocco" Valenti and Silva Tagliagamba, who eventually died of his wounds from the gunfight. Valenti was one of New York City's top hit men at the time, and the assassination attempt was ordered by Masseria rival and Brooklyn mob kingpin Salvatore D'Aquila.

In retaliation, Valenti was killed on August 11, 1922, farther up Second Avenue, and D'Aquila was gunned down on October 10, 1928, on Avenue A.

### 87 Second Avenue

On July 19, 1981, career criminal Jack Henry Abbott stabbed twenty-two-year-old restaurant worker Richard Adan to death on the sidewalk here, in front of what used to be the Binibon Café. This murder gained national headlines because of Abbott's relationship with novelist and socialite Norman Mailer.

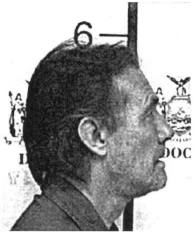

Jack Henry Abbott.

Jack Henry Abbott was in and out of prison for the better portion of his life. Abbott had racked up multiple murder and felony convictions, including a brief escape from Utah State Penitentiary.

In 1978, Norman Mailer was in the midst of researching and writing *The Executioner's Song*, a novel about a death-row inmate, when he formed a relationship with Abbott. They continued correspondence for four years, and Abbott eventually sent Mailer a manuscript for his prison-penned novel, *In the Belly of the Beast*. Mailer was so fond of Abbott and his book that he not only got the book published, but he also petitioned the parole board to release Abbott from prison. Abbott was placed in a local halfway house and given a job at a publishing company.

On the morning of July 19, while Jack Henry Abbott was having breakfast here at the Binibon, he asked Richard Adan for directions to the restroom. Unfortunately for Adan, the Binibon either did not have a restroom or it was under construction, but as the account goes, Adan asked Abbott to follow him outside, where he would be shown where to "relieve himself." For no known reason, Abbott

# East Houston Street to East Fourteenth Street:
## A Radical New Direcation

Norman Mailer. *Courtesy of the Library of Congress, Prints & Photographs Division, Carl Van Vechten Collection.*

pulled out a knife, stabbed Adan multiple times and fled. Because Abbott was so high profile, he was spotted and caught a few weeks later while hiding out in Louisiana. He was sent right back to prison for manslaughter.

There is one ironic twist to this story. On the very same morning of the murder, the *New York Times* published a glowing review of Abbott's book that also praised Norman Mailer for discovering this untapped talent. "Out of nowhere comes an exceptional man with an exceptional literary gift. His voice is like no other, his language is sharp-edged and hurling with rage."

Norman Mailer was no stranger to controversy. He stabbed his wife with a penknife in 1960 and spent seventeen days in a mental institution. He was married six times.

## 140 Second Avenue

What is now the Ukrainian National Home and restaurant was
once Stuyvesant Hall, a popular meeting hall, restaurant and
ballroom where politicians, unions and gangsters alike would hold
social events at the turn of the century.

At an event here in the summer of 1911, small-time criminals
Albert Rooney and Domenick Martello got into a heated argument.
Rooney left to retrieve a weapon and then returned and waited
in the shadows of the hallway to ambush Martello. As Martello
entered the vestibule, Rooney shot him three times in the back.
One shot sliced his spinal column in half.

On December 6, 1911, "Big" Jack Zelig held an event here at
Stuyvesant Hall for his associates under the pseudonym "the Boys
of the Avenue."

Rival gang member Jules Morello was an uninvited and inebriated
guest who intended to kill Zelig on behalf of Jack Sirocco and
Chick Tricker, former Zelig partners who were making a power
play for his empire.

Jules Morello, who was reported to be "staggeringly drunk,"
made his way upstairs toward the ballroom, reportedly yelling,
"Where is that Yid? I'm gonna get that Yid!"

Zelig appeared at the top of the steps and fired, hitting Morello
four times. Morello staggered out of the hall and collapsed on the
sidewalk, dying from his injuries. No one was ever convicted of
the murder.

## 142 Second Avenue

The building that now hosts Veselka Diner was, in the early
twentieth century, an all-night café and casino named the
Boulevard, which was commonly referred to as Dutchman's after
its owner's nickname.

On April 10, 1937, at three o'clock in the morning, four
neighborhood boys, Arthur Friedman, Dominick Guariglia, Philip

Chaleff and Joseph Harvey O'Laughlin, entered the café with the intentions of robbing it.

What was thought to be an easy heist turned into a fierce and deadly gun battle. Inside, two of the patrons happened to be plainclothes officers, Detectives Michael Foley and John Gallagher, who were enjoying a coffee break at a table with the Dutchman himself.

Guariglia yelled, "This is a stick up!" He and Friedman were herding patrons into the kitchen in the back when the gun battle erupted.

Instead of complying, the detectives went for their guns and both sides exchanged fire. O'Laughlin managed to fire a round that eventually killed Detective Foley but took a shot to the chest and arm before escaping out the front door with Chaleff. Detective Foley, though severely wounded, managed to corral Friedman and Guariglia in the kitchen until back-up arrived; the boys were unaware that Foley's weapon was empty the whole time.

O'Laughlin and Chaleff were captured within hours, along with an accomplice, Isidore Immerman, who helped plan the robbery. O'Laughlin, Friedman and Guariglia were executed at Sing Sing prison, while Chaleff and Immerman received life sentences.

## *152–154 Second Avenue*

In June 1953, services for accused and executed spies Julius and Ethel Rosenberg were held here at the Gramercy Park Memorial funeral home (which just moved in 2007). The Rosenbergs lived and were raising their son at 103 Avenue A up until the time of their federal trial for selling atomic secrets to the Soviet Union.

Julius Rosenberg was born on May 12, 1918, in New York City to Polish immigrant parents and moved to the Lower East Side by age eleven. He graduated from Seward Park High School when he was sixteen. Ethel Greenglass was also born in New York City, on September 28, 1915. The two met as teenagers while members of the Young Communist League.

Julius and Ethel Rosenberg.

## *156 Second Avenue*

On the morning of March 4, 1996, Holocaust survivor and beloved community member Abe Lebewohl was murdered in an unsolved robbery while opening his store for business. Lebewohl opened the Second Avenue Kosher Deli in 1954, and it soon became a magnet for stars of theatre and food aficionados alike. A family member took over the business after the murder but lost its lease in 2007, prompting a move to Third Avenue and Thirty-third Street.

My uncle worked in the kitchen of the Second Avenue Deli as a young man in the 1960s.

## *Intersection of Second Avenue and East Thirteenth Street*

On October 5, 1912, while hanging out at Segal's Café at 76 Second Avenue, "Big" Jack Zelig received a mysterious phone call summoning him to Fourteenth Street. Zelig jumped on a Second Avenue streetcar heading uptown. As the car passed this intersection, small-time criminal "Boston Red" Phil Davidson came up behind Zelig and fired one shot at point-blank range, striking Zelig behind the ear and killing him instantly. Davidson ran from the scene, heading east on Fourteenth Street, where he was apprehended by a police officer on beat patrol.

The murder of Jack Zelig sparked a controversy that is still being explored today. Davidson claimed that he was getting revenge on Zelig for roughing him up a few days earlier. But many experts believe that Zelig was murdered to prevent his testimony in the upcoming Becker-Rosenthal murder trial. Police lieutenant Charles Becker apparently contracted out Zelig to arrange the assassination of Herman "Beansy" Rosenthal, a West Side gambling-parlor owner who complained to the media and district attorney about Becker's shakedowns. Just hours after a meeting with the DA, Rosenthal was gunned down on West Forty-third Street. Becker was eventually found guilty of arranging Rosenthal's murder and was electrocuted at Sing Sing prison in 1915. Harry "Gyp the Blood" Horowitz and "Lefty" Louis Rosenberg met the same fate a year prior for their role in the murder.

### Second Avenue between Thirteenth and Fourteenth Streets

The open field that used to occupy this space served as a public execution square, where at least one high-profile hanging took place in the early 1800s, the execution of John Johnson in March 1824. It is reported that fifty thousand people (or about one-quarter of New York City's population) attended the event.

Johnson was the landlord of a boardinghouse on Front Street when Merchant Marine James Murray arrived and asked Johnson a favor. Murray did not trust his shipmates not to steal his chest full of treasure during their stay, so Johnson offered Murray a "safe" place to stay—his own apartment.

The next morning, Murray was found bludgeoned to death, and both Johnson and the treasure were gone.

Johnson was tracked down, tried, convicted and executed. The large turnout at his execution was probably due to a growing anti-landlord sentiment spreading in the city.

## 226 Second Avenue

This was home to "Dopey" Fein gang member Rubin Kaplan at the time of his involvement in the shootout at 19–21 St. Mark's Place in 1914, in which he was charged with murder.

# First Avenue

## 3 First Avenue

In the mid-nineteenth century, this was home to Madame Widger, a successful witch and fortuneteller. Madame Widger set up shop here after settling a series of lawsuits in her hometown of Albany, New York, that left her with some bad publicity.

## 36 First Avenue

On September 20, 1905, a barbershop located here owned by Salvatore Scarlito was blown up by dynamite after Scarlito failed to comply with a Black Hand threat. On March 3. 1907, the *New York Times* published an article about the growing Black Hand tactics used to extort money from local residents and merchants, stating that in just a few years, over three hundred Black Hand–related murders had taken place across the country and local police were responding to as many as thirty-five threats a day. Dozens of New York City businesses were blown up during this time period for failure to pay the extortion, and numerous assaults, stabbings and kidnappings were reported.

A Black Hand threat begins when a very short handwritten note with a dollar amount and date is delivered to an individual or business. The note is always stamped with the "Mano Nera" emblem, which is literally an image of a black hand, sometimes with a knife through its palm or images such as skulls, nooses or handguns. If the fee is not paid on or before the date requested, the uncooperative victim almost always meets with extreme violence.

Large-scale threats existed as well. In many cases, the Black Hand would extort entire gangs of laborers who worked on public works projects like railroads and building construction sites. A Black Hand "key" would sign up to work on the project to pretend to be a victim of extortion, telling his fellow laborers that the Black Hand wanted money from each and every one of them as well. If any of the men did not pay the one-dollar-a-week request, they would be served with a letter asking for fifteen to twenty dollars. If they did not pay that amount, they were often killed or violently assaulted. To say the least, this tactic proved successful, and many laborers paid without delay.

## *79–81 First Avenue*

This was the site of the old Seventeenth Police Precinct back in the mid- to late 1800s.

In 1853, the precinct headquarters were moved from the Bowery and East Third Street to this location on First Avenue. The Seventeenth Precinct patrolled the neighborhood between Fourteenth Street and Houston Street, north to west, and the Bowery to Avenue B, west to east.

The precinct force consisted of seventy-five police officers. There were fourteen day patrolmen and twenty-six night patrolmen who walked the beat. Police were also assigned to specific posts on a daily basis—two men at Cooper Union, one man at Tompkins Square Park, one man at the New York Eye and Ear Infirmary and one man at the home of the Holly family.

The commanding officer through much of the late 1800s was Captain John H. McCullagh, an Irish immigrant who moved to New York City with his family at the age of eleven. At twenty-one years old, he joined the police force after befriending some police officers during the deadly Draft Riots of 1863. McCullagh quickly earned a reputation as a hands-on, rough-and-tumble but likable patrolman, which helped him rise through the ranks in just a few years. He was sort of the Rudy Giuliani of the era, shutting down gangs and arresting some of the city's most violent criminals.

McCullagh suffered a few battle scars along the way. Early in his career, he was shot and severely wounded by a disgruntled ex–police officer after McCullagh had him dismissed from the force. During the Orange Riots of 1871, McCullagh was shot in the leg in the frenzy.

### 155 First Avenue

In the nineteenth century, this was home to a dogfighting ring operated by James McLaughlin. Police raided the establishment on May 28, 1855, and interrupted a violent contest between two bulldogs. Everyone inside the building who was connected to the fights was arrested and given $280 bail.

### 176 First Avenue

According to neighborhood legend, Lucky Luciano and Meyer Lansky were regular patrons of the one-hundred-year-old DeRobertis Pastry shop early in their careers. They would sit at a quiet table in the back, sipping on espressos while discussing business.

In the 1980s, Gambino crime family member Jack Giordano allegedly set up shop here, prompting surveillance by the FBI. John Gotti was said to stop in for discreet meetings and a pastry or two.

# Avenue A

### Tompkins Square Park, Avenue A between East Seventh and East Tenth Streets

Originally swampland, Tompkins Square Park was graded and landscaped between 1835 and 1850, essentially to attract a wealthy population east with the promise of a 10.5-acre open space and waterfront views. Things did not work out as planned, however. With the sprawling settlement of arriving European immigrants and the Civil War ripping the city apart, plans for an upscale community were put on hold.

For a better part of its history, protests and riots were a fairly regular occurrence on these grounds, most notably the Irish-led Bread Riots of 1857, the Civil War Draft Riots of 1863 and the laborer-led Stonecutter Riots of 1874. There were a lot of poor and desperate people in the area, and this was a large, open space in which to congregate and vent.

When the Civil War began, the park was closed to the public, leveled and turned into a parade ground for the National Guard. In 1878, Tompkins Square Park was redesigned by Robert Moses. It went on to serve the surrounding working-class population for the next century.

By the 1970s and '80s, the city was bankrupt, and lower-income areas like the Lower East Side, the South Bronx and inner Brooklyn suffered great cuts in municipal services, education and police protection. Schools were closing, garbage was piling up and crime was increasing, so many families fled to the suburbs.

As much as 30 percent of what many refer to as "Alphabet City" (Avenues A through D) was abandoned, there was an average of twenty-five arson fires a month and the neighborhood earned the dubious distinction of being named the "retail heroin capitol of the world."

The Tompkins
Square riot of 1857.

During this time, Tompkins Square Park (among many other open spaces) became an encampment for hundreds of indigent and impoverished men and women, earning the name Tent City.

After midnight on August 6, 1988, the police department, by orders of Mayor David Dinkins, charged into the park on horseback and forcibly removed every person from the park and vicinity. Possibly hundreds of people were injured in the mêlée, including innocent bystanders, protesters and journalists. It became known as the Tompkins Square Police Riot, and it was the start of an official "cleanup" of the neighborhood.

The park was once again closed and redesigned in 1992. The famous band shell, which hosted performances by Jimi Hendrix, the Grateful Dead and others, was destroyed; a dog run, two playgrounds and other family-oriented amenities were added.

## *211 Avenue A*

Brooklyn-based crime boss Salvatore "Toto" D'Aquila was shot dead here on October 10, 1928, during a hit commonly thought to have been ordered by Giuseppe Masseria.

D'Aquila was escorting his wife Marianna to a doctor's appointment at this address. When he stepped outside to get some fresh air, he was assassinated on the street.

Salvatore "Toto" D'Aquila was a powerful gang leader with ties to such notable crime figures as Frankie Yale and Johnny Torrio. D'Aquila made several power plays in the first couple decades of the century to control much of the Mafia operations in New York City. But by the late 1920s, D'Aquila started to run into trouble. A series of killings targeting D'Aquila's top associates during a war with Giuseppe Masseria left him almost powerless.

Masseria decided not to take any chances and ordered three gunmen to meet D'Aquila outside this address, where he was gunned down in a hail of nine bullets.

# Avenue B

## *29 Avenue B*

Punk rock vocalist and performance artist G.G. Allin was found dead of a heroin overdose in a friend's apartment in this building on June 28, 1993. Allin (born Jesus Christ Allin in Lancaster, New Hampshire) was known for his outrageous and disturbing behavior onstage. He would often consume his own urine and excrement (if he wasn't throwing it at the audience), cut and maim himself and sometimes physically and sexually attack audience members.

In 1993, as a guest on the *Geraldo* TV show, Allin stated, "My body is a rock and roll temple; my flesh, blood and fluid is a communion for the people."

Allin's plan to kill himself onstage never materialized. On the night of his death, he was seen roaming the streets, bloodied and smeared with excrement, after a failed concert at a local dive. He reportedly trashed the venue after some technical difficulties during the band's set. He wound up at an apartment here, where he overdosed and died. Fans actually came by and took pictures with Allin's corpse; his death was not reported until almost twenty-four hours later.

Allin was buried in a leather jacket and jockstrap, with a bottle of whiskey and a microphone. His friends and fans partied, drank and came to the funeral dressed as zombies and corpses—just as Allin wanted.

## *143 Avenue B*

This seventeen-story building named the Christadora House was built in 1928 as a settlement house and community center for struggling immigrants. Besides providing food, shelter, health services and education, the building sported a gym, swimming pool, theatre and recital hall.

In the 1950s, this was home to the Department of Welfare Division of Daycare offices, where hundreds of local children were served.

During the 1960s, the Christadora House housed the Tompkins Square Community Center. In 1968, ex-convict Robert S. Collier, who was convicted in 1966 for conspiracy to blow up the Statue of Liberty, was hired as head of the recreational program at the center.

In the 1970s, this building served as headquarters for the Black Panthers and several other activist groups and artists, including writer Yuri Kapralov. It was members of a disgruntled group of gang members affiliated with the Black Panthers who turned hoses on the building's electrical system in protest and essentially rendered the building uninhabitable.

In 1986, after sitting abandoned for over a decade, the building was turned into luxury condos and became a catalyst of a sometimes violent anti-gentrification movement.

### *169 Avenue B*

In 1969, hippie guru and drifter-mentor James "Groovy" Hutchinson, along with girlfriend Linda Fitzpatrick, was found bludgeoned to death in the basement of this building. A pair of drifters Hutchinson was trying to help turned on him and murdered the couple as they slept. The newspapers ended up dubbing this the "Groovy murders" and it made headlines nationally.

# East First Street

### *Northwest Corner of East First Street and First Avenue*

On this corner was the Livingston Saloon, where at 9:30 p.m. on September 16, 1903, Monk Eastman and three dozen Eastman gang members shot a man, beginning a five-hour shooting and stabbing rampage through the Lower East Side. They assaulted innocent bystanders, smashed storefront windows and kicked over produce carts in a show of force. One detective commenting on the incident said, "They shot up the town in regular Wild West fashion."

By the end of the night, one man was dead and dozens were injured. Twenty-seven-year-old Michael Donavan was shot in the mouth on the corner of Forsyth and Stanton Streets; he died an hour later of his wounds. Others were shot at random places throughout the Lower East Side and attacked with various weapons like blackjacks and billy clubs. Eastman was arrested, but charges were dropped due to "lack of witnesses."

This was often the case for Monk Eastman (born Edward Osterman in Brooklyn, New York, about 1873), one of the most influential gang leaders of the era. Eastman was arrested numerous times during his heyday but was not convicted because he had the support of the great political machine, Tammany Hall. Any time Eastman was arrested, Tammany Hall lobbyists would intervene, allowing Eastman to walk free, often within hours.

# East Second Street

## *67 East Second Street*

This tenement building once served as headquarters for radical antiwar activists Sam Melville and Jane Alpert. Their group was responsible for setting off eight bombs around New York City in the summer of 1969 in protest of the Vietnam War.

Sam Melville (born Samuel Joseph Grossman in 1934) was one of the most influential radicals of the era, having ties to both the Weather Underground and the Black Panthers. Melville met New York City native Jane Lauren Alpert while she was attending Columbia University. They began a romantic and dangerous relationship, plotting the destruction of some of New York City's corporate elite.

They executed a series of bombings throughout the summer and fall of 1969—on July 27, they bombed Grace Pier, owned by the United Fruit Company; on August 20, the Marine Midland Building; on September 19, the Federal Office Building at Federal Plaza; on October 7, the Army Induction Center on Whitehall Street and the Standard Oil offices in the RCA Building; on November 11, the Chase Manhattan Bank headquarters and the General Motors Building; and on November 12, the New York City Criminal Courts Building on Center Street.

All of the targets received warnings prior to the bombing, so casualties were low. The only exception was the Marine Midland attack, which resulted in nineteen injuries.

The group's luck ran out on November 11, just hours after the criminal courthouse bombing, when its members were apprehended while attempting to place bombs around the National Guard Armory on Twenty-sixth Street and Lexington Avenue. They were arrested as part of an FBI sting. A member of the group, George Demmerle, was really an FBI informant who exposed Melville's plans.

Jane Alpert was not part of the group that evening, so when word got back about the arrests, she left town and went underground. Alpert resurfaced in 1974 and turned herself in. She spent two years in prison for her part in the attacks.

In 1970, Sam Melville was standing trial at the federal courthouse when he overpowered an unarmed guard and fled for the exit. He was captured before he left the building and was eventually convicted on multiple charges. He was sentenced to serve time in Attica State Prison. Being a natural radical organizer, he helped plot a prison coup, convincing other prisoners to rise up and take over the prison.

On September 9, 1971, over one thousand prisoners rioted and seized control of the prison, taking thirty-three correction officers hostage. On September 13, New York State Police dropped tear gas into the compound and fired wildly into the mob. By the end of the day, nine hostages and twenty-eight inmates had been killed, including Sam Melville.

# East Houston Street to East Fourteenth Street:
## A Radical New Direcation

Sam Melville.

The New York State Special Commission on Attica wrote:

*With the exception of Indian massacres in the late 19th century, the State Police assault which ended the four-day prison uprising was the bloodiest one-day encounter between Americans since the Civil War.*

Melville's influence did not end upon his death. A national group of extreme radical activists formed the Sam Melville–Jonathan Jackson Unit in honor of Melville and Jackson (a black youth who was killed while attempting to kidnap a California judge). That group evolved into the notorious United Freedom Front. The Melville-Jackson Unit was responsible for seven bombings and one attempted bombing from April 1976 to February 1979. The United Freedom Front claimed responsibility for ten bombings and one attempted bombing between December 1982 and September 1984.

## 171 East Second Street

On February 7, 1966, police found heroin addict Robert Friede outside this building asleep at the wheel in his idling car. Upon inspection, they found the body of nineteen-year-old Celeste Crenshaw in the trunk, wrapped in a blanket.

Crenshaw had died thirteen days earlier of a heroin overdose, administered by boyfriend Friede in his apartment uptown. His attempts to revive her failed, and two weeks later he decided to move her body upstate.

He was at this address waiting for accomplices to help him with the task, when he nodded off. Police pulled up and suspected that Friede was under the influence of heroin, so they searched his vehicle and made the gruesome discovery.

The case caused a national sensation when it was discovered that Robert Friede was an heir to one of America's wealthiest families. (He was grandson to publishing mogul Moe Annenberg.)

The public could not get enough. Headlines like "Society Girl's Body Found in Heir's Car on East Side" and "The Frozen Body of Girl Student in Car of Annenberg Heir" covered newspapers across the country.

Friede pleaded guilty to second-degree manslaughter and was sentenced to two and a half to five years in prison for a parole violation. His manslaughter charges were dropped.

This story was actually significant in bringing national attention to the growing popularity of recreational drugs among America's youth. Once considered part of a subculture, drugs like heroin, LSD and marijuana were beginning to creep into university campuses and gated communities to the alarm of many conservatives.

# East Third Street

*57 Great Jones Street (West of the Bowery, East Third Street
Turns into Great Jones Street)*

At the turn of the century, seminal Five Points gang leader and
founder Paul Kelly ran the Little Naples restaurant here, also
known as the New Brighton Athletic Club. This was the public
headquarters and recreational venue for the most powerful gang in
new York City.

The two-thousand-plus-member Five Points Gang bred a couple
generations of some of the most infamous gangsters in history.
Johnny Torrio, Jack Sirocco, Frankie Yale, Lucky Luciano and Al
Capone, to name just a few, all spent time with the Five Points
gang. Even notorious Jewish mobsters like Max Zwerbach, Nathan

Frankie Yale.

149

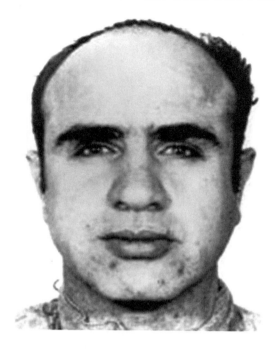

A young Al Capone.

Kaplan and Ritchie Fitzpatrick pledged allegiance to the Five Points gang at one time.

Sicilian immigrant Paul Kelly (born Paulo Vaccarelli in 1876, died in 1936) founded the Paul Kelly Association after a successful career as a professional prizefighter, during which he changed his name to Kelly because having an Irish name gave him more title opportunities.

Paul Kelly did not fit the stereotypical gangster character of the time. He was said to be soft spoken and jovial. He was slight in stature and wore expensive, tailored clothing. He taught himself three languages and kept on top of current affairs. He was a charming criminal who used as much "schmooze" as he did muscle to work his way to the top of the criminal underworld.

On September 3, 1905, an off-duty police officer and one of his friends were beaten, stomped and robbed by Paul Kelly associates while attending an event here at the New Brighton.

# East Houston Street to East Fourteenth Street:
## A Radical New Direcation

On November 23, 1905, four (brave) members of the Liberty Association, a rival gang, entered the nightclub and taunted the crowd. More than a dozen guns were drawn, and innocent patron W.E. Harrington of 56 East First Street was killed in the mêlée, shot in the chest by the dance-floor bar.

In April 1905, police raided the New Brighton Athletic Club, arresting several members of the gang, including Paul Kelly. Four patrolmen testified against Paul Kelly and his association, but a police captain named Bourke, who was in the pocket of the gangster and his political connections, testified, "I have been there [New Brighton] myself, and I can say that I never saw anything out of the way going on there." Court Magistrate Barlow then asked Captain Bourke, "Then you give the place a good character?" to which Bourke replied, "I certainly do." The judge then slammed the gavel and yelled "Dismissed!" to the cheer of five hundred spectators, who were Kelly supporters.

In November 1908, two gunmen, "Biff" Ellison and "Razor" Riley, walked into the New Brighton and casually proceeded to a table at which Paul Kelly was sitting with two bodyguards, Bill Harrington and "Rough House" Hogan.

When they were only ten feet away, Ellison and Riley pulled out two revolvers and shot at the seated gangsters. Harrington yelled, "Look out boss!" and threw Kelly under the table. Harrington took a bullet to the brain for his bravery and died instantly. Kelly came up from under the table with two revolvers blazing and then the lights went out in the hall (a common practice when shootouts begin). Unrelated patrons scurried for the exits under the hail of bullets. In the end, all parties were injured. Ellison and Riley escaped with a few scars, and Kelly was shot three times.

Riley holed himself up in a Chinatown basement and died of pneumonia before the police or Kelly could find him. Ellison was finally tracked down and captured in 1911. He went insane in prison and died in a mental institution a short time later.

Paul Kelly never really recovered after the incident. The New Brighton was ordered to close by police, and Paul Kelly moved

to Harlem, where his involvement in crime and command of the
underworld eventually dwindled.

## 77 East Third Street

This is the New York City chapter headquarters of the legendary
Hells Angels Motorcycle Club, dating back to 1969.

Since its modest beginnings in Fontana/San Bernardino,
California, in 1948, public fascination with this outlaw biker group
has continued to grow along with the club itself, branching out to
dozens of countries over the past several decades.

The most organized group of its kind, the Hells Angels boasts
possibly thousands of members around the globe, including those
in Europe, South America, Australia and South Africa, but for a
period of time in the 1970s and '80s, the New York City chapter
was known as one of the most respected and formidable in the
entire organization.

The FBI has classified the Hells Angels as a "criminal syndicate,"
claiming that the organization is heavily involved in everything
from international drug trafficking to extortion, yet members
contend that they are simply law-abiding motorcycle enthusiasts
who get a bad rap for the actions of a few rogue members. Hells
Angels chapters are routinely involved in toy drives, fundraisers
and various charity work in the cities they occupy, yet there is no
denying the countless newspaper reports and accounts of violence
that have both tarnished and elevated the organization's reputation
since the infamous Altamont incident in 1969, when an audience
member was killed during a fight with the Angels during a Rolling
Stones performance.

It is no coincidence that Third Street is known as the "safest
block in the city." I know firsthand, as I have lived directly across the
street from them for several years, that they make great neighbors;
that is, if you can deal with a pack of Harley Davidson motorcycles
roaring through the narrow street on a daily basis. You can hear
them coming from blocks away—it's like a jet plane landing on

your roof. You are practically thrown out of your bed as car alarms from surrounding blocks are triggered by the shaking earth.

I recall a few clubhouse Fourth of July parties that would last for days. The Hells Angels had all the vehicles removed from the block (not necessarily by obtaining proper permits) to make room for Angels from around the world. Hundreds of Angels invaded the city, with "rockers" from places as far away as Germany. (A rocker is a patch on the back of the vests that identifies the wearer's origin.) They would celebrate until all hours of the night, setting off fireworks, doing wheelies up and down the block and engaging in general nonviolent debauchery. It was quite an intimidating sight, which is what the Hells Angels are all about—being the biggest, baddest, most intimidating crew on two wheels. Their reputation alone is enough to deter most challengers, and those who make the attempt are met with swift and severe consequences.

I have personally witnessed incidents of alcohol-inspired rowdies challenging the sanctity of the block and the legend of the club—and I can tell you, factually, that the Hells Angels are undefeated. Many altercations that started with, "You're not so tough" ended with a trip to the hospital for the antagonist.

As far as this club chapter is concerned, if you don't mess with them and respect their privacy, they do not mess with you. Despite their fearsome reputation, these Angels do not go around terrorizing people and only react in violence when provoked.

The New York City chapter of the Hells Angels was chartered here on December 5, 1969, by Sandy Frazier Alexander. Alexander arrived in New York City in 1967, after serving the country in the United States Marine Corps. Back in California, he was a Hells Angels "hang around" (the first of many steps in becoming a full-fledged club member). Upon arriving in the city, Alexander pledged as a member of the Alien Motorcycle Club, which had chapters in every borough of New York by the late 1960s.

Alexander quickly realized that the Aliens were not "true outlaws"—he said that they only worked for the mob, not for themselves, and he wanted more. So he convinced thirteen Alien members to break away and form a chapter under the Nomad Motorcycle Club banner.

In 1968, Alexander and his new Nomad chapter rented the basement here at 77 East Third Street for use as its headquarters.

By 1969, Alexander decided that being a Nomad was still not good enough, so he headed to California to ask the Hells Angels permission to charter a New York chapter. In December of that year, the Nomads officially became Hells Angels. It was only the third Hells Angels chapter on the East Coast.

The new New York City chapter grew powerful very quickly. Alexander's reputation as a ruthless but disciplined and dedicated Angel rivaled that of only one other man, Hells Angels founder Sonny Barger.

One thing that the Hells Angels, and Alexander in particular, despised was injected drugs like heroin. In the minds of the Angels, a heroin user is loyal to the drug, not the club, and cannot be trusted. That was a bit of a problem in the 1970s, when the neighborhood was infested with heroin addicts and drug gangs.

Actually, it was a problem for the dealers and junkies. Angel members routinely "shook down" drug pushers in the neighborhood, roughing them up and stomping their dope into the cement. This block between First and Second Avenues became one of the few blocks in the East Village that was junkie (and crime) free, earning its reputation as "the safest block in New York City." The Angels boasted to the media that they were "more successful than federal authorities at getting heroin off the streets."

On November 23, 1970, the Grateful Dead, Riders of the Purple Sage and Steve Winwood performed a benefit for the Hells Angels at the Anderson Theatre around the corner on Second Avenue. It was billed as "Hells Angels Awakening for the Living," and tickets were only two dollars.

On March 7, 1971, New York City Hells Angels member Jeffrey S. "Groover" Coffey was killed in Cleveland during a brawl between a Hells Angels associate club and a rival motorcycle group called the Akron Breed. This riot left five bikers dead, twenty injured and eighty-four arrested; ten Hells Angels and forty-six Breed members were held on murder charges. During a week-long ceremony for Coffey at this clubhouse, a visiting Hells Angels group allegedly raped and assaulted a seventeen-year-old girl in a local leather goods shop. Eight Angels were arrested, but only one was charged.

The first major raid on this Hells Angels clubhouse took place in March 1972. Five club members were arrested, and an arsenal of "guns, knives and explosive devices" was seized from the premises.

"Big" Vinnie Giorlamo, known as "the Beast from the East," was sergeant of arms of this chapter in the late '70s, when on September 21, 1977, he threw thirty-two-year-old Mary Ann Campbell to her death from the clubhouse roof during a party, reportedly egged and cheered on by other club members. Six-foot, two-inch, 350-pound Giorlamo was not convicted for Campbell's death, and two years later, he died on the operating table after suffering a ruptured kidney in a fight with a fellow Angel. Cards handed out at his burial included Giorlamo's favorite phrase, "When in doubt, knock 'em out," which has become a Hells Angels mantra.

It is suggested that by the late 1970s, the New York chapter of the Hells Angels grew close to the Gambino crime family, providing strong-arm services and getting involved in methamphetamine production and distribution. A local university chemist allegedly taught Sandy Alexander how to manufacture the drug.

On May 10, 1979, refrigerator maintenance man, Golden Gloves boxer and Bronx-born street brawler Chuck Zito was pledged into the New York City chapter as an official Hells Angels member in a ceremony presided over by Sandy Alexander. Charles Alfred "Chuck" Zito was introduced to the club by Vinnie Giorlamo after the two met while shooting pool in the Bronx. At the time, Zito was a member of the Nomad Ching-a-Ling biker club. Zito was well liked and quickly rose through the ranks to become president of the New York Hells Angels in the early 1980s before becoming a bodyguard to some of Hollywood's elite, including Charles Bronson, Mickey Rourke, Bon Jovi, Liza Minnelli and Sylvester Stallone. Zito used his connections to eventually start his own successful film career, most notably playing the role of inmate Chucky Pancamo on the HBO series *Oz*.

In May 1983, club member Larry Van Tassel was shot on East Fourth Street near the Bowery. Off-duty police officer Daniel DiGiorgio accidentally bumped Van Tassel's motorcycle while parking his car, and Van Tassel responded by attacking the officer. While being choked, DiGiorgio drew his weapon and fired once, hitting Van Tassel in the leg.

In 1983, Sandy Alexander co-wrote, co-produced and starred in a big-screen documentary about the club, entitled *Hells Angels Forever*. The movie went on to show in cities across the country and has become somewhat of a cult classic. The film also featured longtime friends of the club like Jerry Garcia and Willie Nelson and was intended to soften the Hells Angels image.

In 1985, a nationally organized raid on the Hells Angels Motorcycle Club resulted in at least 125 arrests; one state trooper was shot in the stomach in a Connecticut raid. This clubhouse was raided on May 2, 1985, and a handful of members were arrested, including Sandy Alexander, who was sentenced to sixteen years in prison. Brendan Manning, a club member who was well liked on both coasts, became president of the New York chapter—and to my knowledge, is still president today.

Three Angels, including founding member William "Wild Bill" Medeiros, testified against the club after making a deal with the government for a reduced sentence. They testified that the Hells Angels were importing and distributing large quantities of amphetamines and had murdered at least two club members suspected of being informants. U.S. attorney Rudolph Giuliani, who headed the sting operation, wore a confiscated Hells Angels vest at a press conference, which outraged club members.

Another raid occurred on August 5, 1999, when fifty New York City police officers entered the building and overstepped their ground-floor warrant by going up the stairs and invading private apartments. The Hells Angels sued and were awarded $450,000 in a civil suit against the city.

## East Houston Street to East Fourteenth Street: A Radical New Direcation

The last raid on this clubhouse occurred just recently. On January 29, 2007, local authorities entered the building armed with automatic weapons while a police helicopter hovered overhead, police tanks with special enforcement units waited outside and snipers perched themselves on rooftops.

Five Angels were taken into custody but released soon after. The front door and surveillance videos were taken away as evidence in a woman's beating the night before. Witnesses allege that the Hells Angels pulled her into the clubhouse off the street after a confrontation at nearby Edge Bar and then beat her unconscious, throwing her lifeless body back out onto the street.

To the misfortune of the police, none of the Angels was convicted of a crime, and the club is now suing the City of New York once again. (The trial has not yet begun at the time of this publishing.)

If you're brave enough to look hard enough, you can actually tell the status and history of each biker by the individual's tattoos and vest patches. Club hit men allegedly have two Nazi SS bolts tattooed under their armpits, accompanied by the words "Filthy Few"; some bikers represent every successful murder on behalf of the club with a skull tattoo that bares black eyes if the victim was a man and red eyes if the victim was a woman. The letters $E$ and $F$, tattooed at a forty-five-degree angle, mean that the biker is part of the "Evil Force," a name thought up by Vinnie Giorlamo to show that you killed a rival Outlaw club biker on behalf of the Hells Angels. The "red badge of courage," which reads "Deguello" in red letters on a white vest patch, means that the club member has violently resisted arrest.

Please note that this is an active clubhouse. The Angels do not mind if you come by for a picture or two of the building, but as a warning, do not try to take a club member's picture, don't get too nosy and, whatever you do, do not touch their motorcycles. If they request that you move on, comply immediately—they only ask once.

### 106 East Third Street

On September 15, 1894, ten-year-old Charles Feig stabbed his thirteen-year-old neighbor John Klein in the heart for refusing to participate in a practical joke.

Ringing doorbells and running was a new fad in the neighborhood, one in which both boys had participated many times in the past. However, on this day, Feig refused, and Klein slapped him in the face as the argument escalated. The younger Feig immediately drew a jackknife and stabbed Klein in the chest. Klein was expected to die of his injuries, and Feig was held on murder charges.

# East Fourth Street

### 59–61 East Fourth Street

This was home to the Metamora Social Club, established in 1900 and said to be composed of friends and members of Paul Kelly's Five Points gang. Members included John McKeon, eighteen years of age, and Antonio Platanio, twenty-three.

By the 1930s, the Astoria Press, a Jewish/Yiddish-themed book publisher, was located in this building. In December 1939, owner Morris Sweder was accused of operating a front for a $10 million narcotics ring allegedly controlled by Louis "Lepke" Buchalter but was never convicted.

### 62 East Fourth Street

This uniquely designed 1889 building served as a union hall early in the century before hosting several theatres in the 1930s and '40s. In the 1960s, Andy Warhol rented out the second-floor theatre to create male hardcore porn films. In 1973, Francis Ford Coppola rented the same theatre to shoot the famous Italian operetta scene from *The Godfather, Part II*.

# East Houston Street to East Fourteenth Street: A Radical New Direcation

## 64 East Fourth Street

On July 23, 1903, Mary Harris, better known as Mother Jones, a famous socialist labor activist, organized hundreds of textile workers at the union hall located here and then marched up to Madison Square.

## 66–68 East Fourth Street

On October 30, 1906, Emma Goldman was prepared to speak here but was arrested, along with ten others, during opening remarks. Goldman was arrested on "criminal anarchy" charges for distributing a copy of *Mother Earth* magazine, which commemorated the fifth anniversary of Leon Czolgosz's execution (the man who assassinated President McKinley). Charges were dropped by a grand jury in 1907.

By the 1920s and '30s, this was home to the Black Bottom nightclub, where, on October 31, 1930, local gangsters "Cowboy Larry" Viscordi and Charles Grecco were gunned down and killed during a fight.

## 71 East Fourth Street

In June 1898, resident Otto Krupp of the U.S. Army First Cavalry Division was killed alongside Hamilton Fish (grandson of U.S. secretary of state Hamilton Fish) in the Battle of La Quasina in Cuba.

Thirty-seven-year-old Otto Krupp was a veteran of various Indian wars in America's West as a member of Teddy Roosevelt's Rough Riders. The Riders saw the most action in the 1898 war against Spain in which Krupp was killed.

Krupp's family continued to live at this address after their son's death and reached out to the family of Hamilton Fish to secure proper arrangements for their son's funeral.

## 85 East Fourth Street

At the turn of the century, this building was used as a union
hall for various labor organizations. From the 1910s through the
1920s, it was called the Royal Hall. In the 1930s, it was called
Mansion Hall.

In October 1910, Herman Liebowitz was lured here, along with
a handful of other strikebreakers, to the headquarters of the Cloak
and Suitmakers Union. Strikers assaulted the small group, and
Liebowitz was beaten to death in the street.

In the 1920s, this building was home to Lucky Luciano's famous
Palm Casino, an exclusive brothel, restaurant and gambling joint
for heavyweights of the criminal world. The KGB bar now occupies
the space on the second floor, which is largely unchanged from the
era of Luciano.

During the production of this book, proprietors discovered
a trapdoor in the basement of 85 East Fourth Street, which led
underground to a neighboring factory two buildings over. The
assumption is that during Prohibition, a supply truck would unload
alcohol in the factory and men would transport it underground into
the Palm Casino.

## 195 East Fourth Street

In January 1868, boarder Peter Lind died here of injuries he
sustained in a New Year's Eve brawl at a saloon on East Fourth Street
and Avenue A. Witnesses say that Lind was struck several times, at
least once in the head with the butt end of a pistol. Cabinetmaker
George Hammel was put on trial for the murder.

## 198, 200 and 202 East Fourth Street

On February 20, 1883, a tragedy occurred here when a panic
caused a stairway railing to collapse, sending fifteen children to
their deaths and injuring a slew of others.

# East Houston Street to East Fourteenth Street:
## A Radical New Direcation

Shortly after three o'clock in the afternoon, a small fire broke out on the staircase between the second and third floors of the Roman Catholic School of the Most Holy Redeemer Church at this location. The fire burned through the classroom walls, sending hundreds of children ranging in age from five to fifteen into the halls. The crush of children on a second-floor stairway proved too much—the pine boards snapped and the children fell to the floor below.

The *New York Times* reported, "The scene was a frightful one. Children, large and small, tumbled one by one headlong into the struggling, shrieking mass. The floor at the bottom of the stairs was piled three and four deep."

## 236 East Fourth Street

In June 1894, a man who claimed to be the rightful heir to the Austrian throne was found living in the coal cellar of this building.

Franz Stanislaus Ritter von Hrubijeleni was found dirty, unshaven and disheveled during a routine inspection and claimed to be the son of Maximilian, emperor of Austria. He explained that he came to the United States after his father was killed and after spending time in a Mexican prison. He was planning on starting a new colony but went broke and found himself living here, where he set up a struggling coal and wood business. Whether he was royalty or not, he was evicted from the basement. He planned on returning to Austria to reinstate his rank among the noblemen.

## 266 East Fourth Street

On September 3, 1900, eighteen-year-old Rebbecca Markowitz was sitting on the curb in front of her home at this address when a misguided skyrocket hit her in the head and killed her.

Rebbecca was with her sister, Elizabeth, and two neighborhood boys, watching a parade in honor of the Louis Kolish Association. A saloon across the street, located at 249 East Fourth Street, was lighting off fireworks in celebration when a parade-goer accidentally knocked the skyrocket's container to the ground, causing it to speed across the street in the direction of Rebbecca Markowitz instead of up in the air.

The owner of the bar, John Probst, was arrested and locked up in the Union Market police station but was later released on bail.

# East Fifth Street

## *221 East Fifth Street*

At the turn of the century, this was the home of Eastman gang leader and founder Monk Eastman.

Monk Eastman practically set the blueprint for the satirized gangster of the twentieth century. By all accounts, he was a semiliterate, bullet head–shaped, no-nonsense brute. His moniker practically says it all; supposedly "Monk" is short for "monkey," a term describing his manners and appearance. At a time when many gangsters dressed and accessorized above their means, Eastman kept true to his working-class roots, often appearing disheveled and unkempt. His face, neck, head, ears and hands were filled with scars and were twisted from multiple fist-, knife and gunfights. His hair was always long for the day and unwashed, with rogue curls sprouting out from under his derby cap (which was said to be too small for his large head).

Eastman had every opportunity to lead a normal, respectful, middle-class life. Since he was an enthusiastic animal lover, his family set him up with a retail pet store to manage on Broome Street when he was about seventeen years old. The business failed because Eastman discouraged shoppers from purchasing the animals he grew attached to.

Monk Eastman began his barbarous career in the nefarious nightlife district of New York City as a bouncer at one of the roughest and most ornery nightclubs on the Lower East Side, the New Irving Social Club on the Bowery.

He quickly gained a reputation as a powerful pugilist and provoked even more fear by carrying a four-foot stick while on duty that bore a notch for every poor victim he hit over the head. Within six months, Eastman's feared bludgeon had forty-nine notches. He was sending so many people to the hospital that Bellevue Hospital staff called the emergency room "Eastman Pavilion" as an inside joke.

This is how Monk Eastman began his rise to power. By injecting himself head- and fist first into the underworld, he drew the attention of politicians and businessmen, who began to hire him out for certain "favors." As the favors grew, so did his army.

At the height of Monk Eastman's power, he was said to employ up to two thousand of the Lower East Side's toughest street thugs, petty criminals, con artists and murderers.

As ruthless as Eastman was, he always had a soft spot for animals. It is said that Eastman kept dozens of cats in his apartment here and dozens of pigeons on the roof. He was often seen walking home with a coat full of rescued kittens, and in an interview he stated, "I'll beat up any guy dat gets gay wit' a kit or a boid in my neck of de woods."

And it appears Eastman did have some compassion for women. He stated that if he had to hit a woman, he would "takes me brass knuckles off" and hit her "just hard enough to give her a shiner."

Monk Eastman's luck finally ran out in 1904, when he was sentenced to ten years in Sing Sing prison after robbing a man on the West Side. Tammany Hall had recently tried multiple times to reign in Eastman's extracurricular activities to no avail, so when Eastman committed this final "unauthorized" crime, Tammany Hall declined to intervene.

## 321 East Fifth Street

This is the infamous "Fighting Ninth," New York City Police Department's ninth precinct. The officers in this precinct were known as being as rough and tumble and eccentric as the neighborhood they patrolled. For the better part of the area's history, crime has been an integral piece of the neighborhood's culture. Until the end of the twentieth century, this precinct had to adapt to, and deal with, organized criminals, deadly street gangs, domestic terrorists, anarchists, activists, hippies, yippies, religious cults, squatter evictions and a drug infestation and homeless crisis that spanned several decades.

Through much of the 1970s and '80s, police were on the front lines of a collapsing economy and corrupt administration.

Being a police officer at the time was a tough and dangerous job. Police were often shot at or would have cement bricks thrown at them from rooftops. Even the most dedicated officers had their hands tied when it came to doing their job—crime was just too overwhelming, and the city did not have the resources to deal with it on any level.

On January 27, 1972, rookie police officers Gregory Foster and Rocco Laurie were standing on the southwest corner of Avenue B and East Eleventh Street when a group of men approached them. The men walked past the officers and then turned and fired eighteen shots into their backs, without provocation and without warning. Both officers were killed, and the gunmen fled.

The gunmen were tied to the Black Liberation Army, a militant splinter group of the Black Panthers, which had headquarters in the East Village. The group felt that the Black Panthers were not aggressive enough in their activism, and these murders were part of a nationwide campaign of violence against police perpetrated by these rogue members.

The ninth precinct has been used as the backdrop in many books, movies and television shows, including *NYPD Blue* and *Kojak*, and at the time of this publishing, HBO was working on a new series called *Last of the 9th* about the precinct and the neighborhood in the early 1970s.

I am proud to say that two of my three police officer uncles served in the ninth precinct—Officer Paul Ratikan and Detective Walter Ratikan.

## East Houston Street to East Fourteenth Street:
### A Radical New Direction

### *420 East Fifth Street*

In 1902, this building housed the offices of Dr. Samuel Landsman, a popular local physician. On March 16 of that year, Dr. Landsman left the office and climbed into a waiting buggy. As the doctor grabbed the reins of the horse, a gunman appeared and, without saying a word, fired a shot at point-blank range toward Landsman's chest.

The shot startled the horses, which made a mad rush up the street. The gunman ran east but was jumped by vigilant neighbors and held for police.

Dr. Landsman survived the attack unscathed, with a bullet hole in the front of his vest. He found the bullet in the lining of his coat.

The gunman, Alois Spinner, was upset that his infant son, who was suffering from meningitis, convulsions and pneumonia, had died under the treatment of Dr. Landsman.

# East Sixth Street

### *325 East Sixth Street*

The Sixth Street Community Synagogue building housed the St. Mark's Evangelical Lutheran Church for the better part of the nineteenth and twentieth centuries.

On June 14, 1904, over thirteen hundred members of the church boarded a wooden steamship, the *General Slocum*, which was chartered to take the congregation on an annual day trip to Bear Mountain in upstate New York.

The events of this fateful voyage were the most disastrous in New York City history up until the attacks of September 11, 2001, and began the decline of Klein Deutschland ("Little Germany") on the Lower East Side.

The ship caught fire about twenty minutes into the voyage as
it passed through the infamously rough waters of Hell's Gate in
the East River. A small fire started in a cabin toward the front
of the ship and quickly spread throughout the freshly painted
wood boat.

Ship captain William H. Van Schiack ignored several warnings
of the fire and refused to land the ship. A series of bad decisions
and horrible oversights of safety led to a terrifying chain of events.
The boat had been freshly painted for an inspection, and much of
the highly flammable paint was not yet dry. In fact, some of the
lifeboats had been placed on deck prematurely, and victims could
not remove them, as the paint had dried and sealed them to the
ship's deck. Other life rafts were in poor condition or tied down
and unobtainable. Life vests were old and decrepit and many fell
apart when applied. Fire hoses cracked and burst from age when
turned on. Three floors of the ship ultimately collapsed, crushing
hundreds. Many passengers jumped into the turbulent waters and
were drowned by the currents.

Captain Van Schiack was eventually charged and convicted on
multiple counts of negligence and manslaughter and sentenced
to prison, but he was pardoned by President William Taft on
December 19, 1912.

# East Seventh Street

### *111 East Seventh Street*

This was the address of small-time criminal "Boston Red" Phil
Davidson. In 1912, he made big-time headlines for killing "the
most feared man in New York," "Big" Jack Zelig. That incident
is discussed later in the tour, at the intersection of Second Avenue
and East Thirteenth Street.

# St. Mark's Place

### *6 St. Mark's Place*

From 1911 to 1915, this was the site of the anarchist institution the Modern School. Modeled after the philosophy of educator and anarchist Francesc Ferrer i Guàrdia, the school intended to "provide education to the working-classes from a liberating, class-conscious perspective."

One of the professors of the Modern School was the great American anarchist and author Emma Goldman, and philosopher Will Durant was principal. Notable Russian-American anarchist and writer Alexander Berkman also gave presentations at the Modern School.

### *8 St. Mark's Place*

On the site of this Italianate-style building (built circa 1889) once stood a four-story row house that housed the offices of Madame Van Buskirk, one of New York City's most infamous abortionists in the 1860s and '70s. In the late 1800s, this poorly regulated procedure was undergoing a drastic change in public opinion. Once never a prominent social topic, abortion began coming under fire because of a series of high-profile and sensationalized cases involving patient deaths. By 1876, abortion had become illegal, Buskirk moved out and Juliete Corson opened the New York Cooking School in the former offices of the abortion clinic.

By the 1880s, the cooking school had moved on, and the space was turned into La Trinacria Italian restaurant, where, in 1888, the first recorded Italian mob hit in America took place. Antonio Flaccomio was stabbed to death by the Quarteraro brothers after a night of drinking and dining at the restaurant. It was the first time that the word "Mafia" made its way into American newspapers.

One of the Quarteraro brothers escaped by boarding a plane to Italy the very next day, disguised as a priest. The other brother was apprehended and stood trial but was never convicted due to lack of witnesses.

## 19–25 St. Mark's Place

Originally separate town houses built in the 1830s, these buildings were combined by the Arion Society as a social club that served the German community in the nineteenth century. The German community had moved on by the first decade of the twentieth century, but the hall continued as a social club and meeting hall for unions and politicians under the name Arlington Hall. Political leaders and businessmen like Theodore Roosevelt and William Randolph Hearst gave speeches here, and in 1914 there was a famous shootout between the "Dopey" Benny Fein gang and the rival Jack Sirocco gang. It was, in the end, a huge failed hit attempt.

Jack Sirocco wanted to flex some muscle and very publicly rented out Arlington Hall for an event in Benny Fein's territory. When Fein found out about this, he was furious and made plans for an ambush.

On the night of January 9, 1914, the Sirocco gang arrived with two carloads of gangsters. As they entered the hallway, nine of Benny Fein's men emerged from the shadows and released a flurry of gunshots at near point-blank range. Sirroco's gang, anticipating trouble, returned fire quickly, and a large gun battle ensued.

Believe it or not, considering the proximity of the participants, neither side struck its targets. Unfortunately, an innocent passerby, a county clerk officer named Frederick Strauss, was shot in the crossfire and killed.

Strauss was the only casualty of what would become a huge embarrassment for Fein, who ended up stepping down as gang leader. He was picked up by police and ratted out many of his colleagues in exchange for a lighter sentence. Fein eventually slipped out of the spotlight altogether to pursue legitimate business opportunities.

# East Houston Street to East Fourteenth Street:
## A Radical New Direcation

### *Second Avenue and St. Mark's Place*

On July 25, 1876, police sergeant James McGloin confronted suspected thief Harry King at this intersection. King shot and killed McGloin and then served a life sentence for the murder.

### *77 St. Mark's Place*

Russian-language Communist newspaper *Novy Mir* was published in the basement of this building early in the twentieth century. Lev Davidovich Bronstein, better known as Leon Trotsky, worked for the paper and lived across the street at 80 St. Mark's Place in 1917.

Leon Trotsky was one of the most iconic revolutionaries of the twentieth century. He was second in command to Lenin during the Russian October Revolution, leader of the Bolshevik Revolution and founder of the Soviet Red Army.

While in New York, Trotsky stayed politically active. In March 1917, Trotsky submitted a proposal to the New York County

Leon Trotsky.

77 St. Mark's Place today.

80 St. Mark's Place today.

Socialist Party to encourage its members to strike against enlistment in World War I. At a party meeting at Lennox Hall, however, the proposal was voted down. A party member stated, "We should be asses to tell members that they must risk death and imprisonment rather than join the army!"

Trotsky left New York City when the Russian Revolution broke out. Later, under Joseph Stalin, he was exiled from the Soviet Union and murdered by a Soviet agent in Mexico.

## *102 St. Mark's Place*

The second floor of this little red tenement building was the site of a shootout between police and a white supremacist terrorist group.

On December 23, 1974, a call was made by a man who claimed that he had been held hostage at this location and had escaped. Police officers Donald Muldoon and Tom Cimler were sent to investigate. Officer Muldoon knocked on the door and was met by a man with a weapon who fired four shots, striking Muldoon in the side and thigh. Both officers returned fire. Emptying their weapons, they struck their assailant nine times, fatally wounding the gunman.

Upon inspection, investigators found a hostage handcuffed in the apartment, an arsenal of weapons, thousands of rounds of ammunition, bomb-making materials, handcuffs, tape and plans to take hostages at the Statue of Liberty. A letter from the group to the FBI vowed, "Every hostage shall die by explosion, automatic fire or drowning."

Muldoon and Cimler were awarded the Combat Cross and continued their work on the police force.

# East Ninth Street

## *700 East Ninth Street*

On August 19, 1989, Daniel Rakowitz stabbed to death, dismembered and ate the remains of nineteen-year-old Monika Beerle inside his apartment in this building. A self-proclaimed religious figure, Rakowitz was a highly visible eccentric character in a neighborhood full of eccentric characters. He often carried around a live chicken, also named Daniel, and professed to have been a reincarnate of Jesus. He started his own religion, called 966, which prayed to marijuana and sacrificed animals.

Monika Beerle was a performance artist and student at the Martha Graham School of Dance, located on Lafayette Street. The

700 East Ninth
Street.

two met that summer and hit it off. She moved into his apartment sixteen days prior to the murder.

Rakowitz bragged about the murder, but since he was known as a storyteller nobody believed him. People became increasingly suspicious when one day he served the homeless of Tompkins Square Park a soup that allegedly contained the remains of Beerle. Police picked up Rakowitz, and he led them to a locker in the Port Authority bus terminal that contained a bucket full of the victim's bleached and boiled bones.

Daniel Rakowitz was found not guilty by reason of insanity and has been locked away in a maximum-security mental institution on Ward's Island ever since. He was denied parole in 2006, despite reports of psychiatric progress and good behavior.

In an autographed photo to the ninth precinct, Rakowitz wrote, "To the Ninth…I'd Love to have you for dinner. [Signed] Dan."

### 820 East Ninth Street

In 1910, Beatrice Kaplan, a relative of Nathan "Kid Dropper" Kaplan, lived here. She was shot twice in the stomach by rival gangster Johnny Spanish after he lured her to a wooded area in Maspeth, Queens.

# East Tenth Street

*First Avenue and East Tenth Street*

In the mid-nineteenth century, this intersection hosted McLaughlin's Bear Pit, where entertainment consisted of "every conceivable gladiatorial contest," from rat v. dog and man v. man to man v. bear and "rat stomping."

*265 East Tenth Street*

This building is where Charles "Lucky" Luciano grew up after his family emigrated from Sicily about 1906 and where he lived until at least 1926. Born Salvatore Luciana in 1897, Luciano is

Charles "Lucky" Luciano.

265 East Tenth Street today.

perhaps the most influential and celebrated gangster in American
history. Unfortunately, not much is reported on his early life, but
it was here on the Lower East Side where Luciano earned his
criminal stripes, formed lifelong criminal relationships and was
groomed to become one of the most powerful men in America
during the early twentieth century.

It seems that ten-year-old Luciano was a bit of a troublemaker,
even back in Sicily. One story claims that he begged an immigration
officer at Ellis Island to change his name, in an attempt to disguise
himself from adversaries from the old country. Within his first year in
New York, Luciano was arrested for shoplifting.

Luciano started his organized crime career while attending a
local public school a few blocks away, where he extorted classmates
for "protection" from being bullied (by Luciano himself). It was
at school that Luciano met classmate Meyer Lansky, a lean but
feisty Jewish boy from Columbia Street who was brave enough to
stand up to Luciano's threats. The two grew to respect each other,
becoming best friends and teaming up for a legendary criminal
career that lasted their entire lives.

Reports say that Luciano was a fairly good student when he
showed up for class, but his chronic delinquency landed him at the
Brooklyn School of Truancy for four months in 1911. He dropped
out of school the following year and applied for working papers at
age fifteen, but after a few seven-dollar-a-week paychecks from a
hat factory, Luciano realized that he wanted more.

Lucky Luciano started hanging out in Mulberry Street
poolrooms, where the locals referred to him as "Salvatore from
Fourteenth Street." He soon found a home among the petty
thugs and ambitious delinquents of Little Italy. It was during this
time when Luciano is said to have become hooked on opium,
after being introduced to the drug by friends in Chinatown. He
started peddling drugs on the streets and getting involved in
petty crimes like burglary and auto theft with childhood friends
Meyer Lansky, Bugsy Seigel and Frank Costello (whom Luciano
met in Harlem).

## East Houston Street to East Fourteenth Street:
## A Radical New Direcation

In 1916, eighteen-year-old Luciano served his first sentence in prison, a six-month stay for heroin possession. After returning to the streets, Luciano caught the attention of Paul Kelly's Five Points gang and was recruited as a full-fledged member. He quickly gained prominence among Five Points veterans like Johnny Torrio and Frankie Yale. Luciano provided muscle for the Five Pointers, and authorities believe that he was responsible for several beatings and murders during this time period on behalf of the gang.

Both Al Capone and Luciano were understudies of Yale and Torrio during their days in the Five Points gang. Eventually, Capone followed Torrio out to Chicago, but Luciano stayed behind in New York, where he continued to be a thug-for-hire while expanding his drug-smuggling and prostitution empire. It was his time in the Five Points gang that taught Luciano the politics of organized crime, and he was a quick study, rising through the ranks and gaining notoriety among the criminal elite. By the end of the 1910s, Luciano had forged relationships with such heavyweights as Arnold Rothstein, Louis "Lepke" Buchalter and Dutch Schultz. (Both Rothstein and Buchalter were born on Henry Street.)

In 1919, the passing of the Volstead Act (Prohibition) created a whole new frontier in American criminality. The Five Points gang had long since dissolved, and small and mid-level criminals were now making fortunes by supplying illegal alcohol to the masses. Everyone wanted a piece of the pie. Twenty-two-year-old Luciano (still known as Salvatore Luciana) essentially looked over the field of contenders and threw his hat behind Giuseppe "the Boss" Masseria, feeling that he had a better chance at winning the multiple wars that were breaking out for control of the alcohol supply. By this time, Luciano was a rising star in New York City's underworld. Masseria took on Luciano with pride, making him his lieutenant and right-hand man, even considering him a son.

Luciano and fellow gangsters like Thomas Lucchese, Frank Costello and Vito Genovese felt restricted by Masseria's old-school tactics. Masseria denied Luciano the right to work with longtime friends such as Meyer Lansky and Bugsy Seigel (who were Jewish) and Frank

Costello (who was from mainland Italy). In Masseria's world, you were not allowed to work with anyone who did not have full Sicilian blood.

By 1929, Luciano grew restless and felt too constricted by Masseria's ancient ideals. He started to explore the idea of an overthrow and became more brazen in his dealings with "outsiders." It was at this same time that Luciano was picked up off the street at gunpoint, put in the trunk of a limousine and driven out to Staten Island, where he was gagged, beaten, stabbed and had his throat slit. Of course, he survived the ordeal and soon officially changed his name to Luciano. In true mobster fashion, Luciano went to the grave without ever revealing the identity of the men who tried to kill him, and to this day there are many theories about who ordered the assassination. Many people believe that it was his own boss, the man who called Luciano a son, Giuseppe Masseria, as a signal to other underlings he sensed were thinking of overthrowing him. Others believe that the assassination was ordered by rival bootlegger Salvatore Maranzano as part of the escalating Castellamarese War between Sicilian-American factions.

Either way, in 1931 Luciano and company jumped ship to Maranzano's family and assassinated Masseria in a Coney Island restaurant. However, after a few months of working for Maranzano, they realized that they hated him even more than Masseria. Maranzano was a university-educated, old-world traditionalist who demanded strict discipline, loyalty and order from his men. In no way did this fit in with Luciano's plan for the future, so yet another rebellion was planned. When Maranzano caught wind of the fact that a mutiny was brewing within his ranks, he ordered a hit out on Lucky Luciano and several others.

On September 10, 1931, Luciano was invited to Maranzano's office, where Vincent "Mad Dog" Coll was hired to assassinate him. But Luciano was one step ahead of his boss, sending four men, including Samuel "Red" Levine, to Maranzano's office pretending to be federal agents. When Maranzano let his guard down, Luciano's men shot and stabbed him to death—even passing Luciano's hired murderer in the hallway on the way out of the office. This move secured Luciano's position as a pillar of the American Mafia over the next several decades.

In the 1940s, Luciano was sentenced to thirty to fifty years in prison for running a multimillion-dollar prostitution ring. Before cutting a deal with the U.S. government securing his early release, Luciano allegedly put out a hit on Nazi leader Adolph Hitler from his jail cell in upstate New York. This was not necessarily done out of compassion for the Jews of Europe, but Luciano figured that the earlier the war was over, the earlier he would be released from prison. Joe Adonis and Thomas Lucchese were summoned by Luciano to the prison and told, "If somebody could knock off this son of a bitch [Hitler], the war would be over in five minutes." He ordered old friend Vito Genovese, in exile in Italy, to do the job. Unfortunately, Genovese was arrested and put in prison before the plan had a chance to materialize.

Luciano was released from prison in 1946, under the condition that he not stay in the United States. Exiled to Italy, Luciano died of a heart attack on January 26, 1962, in Naples International Airport on his way to meet a movie producer.

# East Eleventh Street

### *Corner of East Eleventh Street and Second Avenue*

On September 31, 1922, forty-year-old bootlegger Ignazio La Barbera was shot dead by two rivals. An innocent bystander (and local shoemaker) was shot in the foot during the incident. A set of keys on La Barbera's body led police to a storefront at 321 East Eleventh Street, where they found thirty-nine five-gallon tubs of alcohol and various distillery equipment.

### *303 East Eleventh Street*

The first murder in New York City in which a getaway car was used took place here on April 29, 1910. Gangster Spanish Louis was killed by rival gang members outside of this apartment, and the killers sped away in a Pierce Arrow.

Spanish Louis was a member of the Humpty Jackson gang, a small group of roughs and petty criminals who held meetings in a graveyard on Thirteenth Street. Louis was perhaps one of the most intimidating characters of the era. He was said to be well over six feet tall and lanky, with dark eyes, hair and complexion (which he claimed was attributed to his Spanish roots). No matter what time of year, Louis would wear a black turtleneck, a long black trench coat and a large black sombrero that was wider than his broad shoulders. He was quite an imposing figure.

There was a claim that "Big" Jack Zelig was behind the murder, but no one was ever convicted.

## 332 East Eleventh Street

On January 2, 1908, a Black Hand threat led to the bombing of this building, wrecking the first couple floors, tearing down walls, shattering windows and injuring many residents.

## 416 East Eleventh Street

On April 20, 1907, a banker residing at this address named Salvatore Geinovese received a suspicious package at his doorstep. Having recently been sent a Black Hand extortion note, Geinovese wisely notified authorities of the package. When the Bureau of Combustibles investigated, they found undetonated explosives.

## 507 East Eleventh Street

For nearly a decade in the 1980s, this building was called "the Rock" and was headquarters to local drug kingpin Alejandro Lopez. Lopez made over $4 million a year selling heroin and crack on the Lower East Side. In 1988, police raided the Rock and found the building customized to include solid steel doors, escape hatches and a nightclub. Lopez was sentenced to over thirty-three years in prison.

### East Eleventh Street and Avenue D

On April 13, 1903, one of the century's most sensational early murder cases involved Benedetto Madonia, whose tortured and mutilated body was found in a barrel on the sidewalk here. Madonia was loosely involved in a counterfeiting scheme, along with prominent mob bosses Giuseppe Morello and Ignazio Lupo, as well as Vito Laduca, Giuseppe De Drino and Tomasso "the Ox" Petto.

About a year before the murder, a five-dollar-bill die had been stolen from the United States Mint in Washington, D.C. Giuseppe De Drino was convicted and sent to Sing Sing prison for copying and passing on bills made from the stolen property. De Drino, Madonia's brother-in-law, was apparently doing business with Lupo and felt that he was owed $10,000, which Lupo failed to pay. Madonia was instructed to meet Lupo and ask for the ten grand—a plot police learned about, prompting them to assign local detectives to trail Lupo. As authorities shadowed Lupo and staked out his headquarters, word came of Madonia's mangled remains found in a barrel at this location. Lupo, Laduca and Petto, along with several other men, were arrested and put in the Tombs, but most were released soon after and no one was immediately charged. About a year later, Laduca was found murdered in Italy, and Petto was stabbed sixty-two times in Wilkes-Barre, Pennsylvania, a hit assumedly ordered by Lupo or Morello in an attempt to halt the investigation in its tracks.

# East Twelfth Street

### 232 East Twelfth Street

On this site was a boardinghouse where George Leroy Parker and Harry Longabaugh (better known as Butch Cassidy and the Sundance Kid)

Butch Cassidy.

hid out for several weeks in 1901. After hiding out, they made their escape by boarding a freighter to South America, where they were eventually killed.

## 302 East Twelfth Street

John's one-hundred-year-old Italian restaurant, a quintessential Lower East Side establishment, has a pretty interesting history. You may recognize the early twentieth-century interior from the numerous movies and television shows that have used John's as a backdrop, including *The Sopranos* and other mob-related shows.

This relationship with the mob is not that far-fetched. On August 11, 1922, Joe Masseria took revenge on an unsuspecting Umberto Valenti here.

Three days after Masseria escaped a failed hit attempt by Umberto Valenti, he devised a plan to retaliate and feigned interest in joining forces with Valenti. They met here at John's, where they shook hands. Masseria gave the signal, stepped aside and "between six and a dozen men" emerged from the shadows and gunned Valenti down. Lucky Luciano himself delivered the fatal shots. Two innocent bystanders, including a street sweeper and an eight-year-old girl, were injured in the hail of bullets—but once again, no witnesses were found so no one was ever prosecuted.

## 331 East Twelfth Street

The cemetery that used to occupy this lot was a morbid hangout of the Humpty Jackson gang.

## East Houston Street to East Fourteenth Street:
## A Radical New Direcation

### *343 East Twelfth Street*

On November 26, 1907, a bomb intended for a resident named T. Bonano shattered "every window above the first floor of 343 and 345" East Twelfth Street. Bonano had been receiving threatening Black Hand notes prior to the bombing.

### *413 East Twelfth Street*

On April 29, 1913, a tailor named Frank Sallo, who resided at 406 East Twelfth Street, was walking by this address when an unidentified gunman stepped from the dark hall and fired two shots into the back of his head. There was no known motive for the murder, and the assailant was not captured at the time of the report.

### *635 East Twelfth Street*

Campos Plaza housing complex is named after Dr. Pedro Albizu Campos, a Puerto Rican politician, independence fighter and president of the island's Nationalist Party.

Campos spent much of his adult life in prison on conspiracy charges, where he claims that he was subjected to forced radiation experiments. There is speculation that these experiments led to his death of heart failure in 1956 while in prison.

# East Thirteenth Street

### *208 East Thirteenth Street*

Lithuanian-born Emma Goldman (born June 27, 1869, died May 14, 1940), one of the most polarizing figures of the era, lived here. Emma Goldman arrived in America about 1885 at the age of sixteen with her sister, Helena. They settled in upstate New York,

but after a brief marriage, Emma moved to New York City to
become more involved with politics.

Orthodox Jew turned free-thinking revolutionary Goldman began
writing and lecturing after being inspired by such notable anarchists as
Johann Most and Justus Schwab. Goldman met Alexander Berkman
on her first day in the city, at Sachs's Cafe, a popular hangout for
intellectuals and radicals. The two fell in love and ended up involved
in a partnership that lasted for decades to come.

At that fateful first meeting, Berkman invited Goldman
to a lecture that same evening by Johann Most, the publisher
of the radical magazine *Die Freiheit* and a leading advocate of
American *propagande par le fait* ("propaganda of the deed"—using
violence against political forces that hold down the working
class). Goldman and Most hit it off immediately, and Goldman
began writing for *Die Freiheit* and giving lectures on behalf of the
growing anarchist movement.

In June 1892, Berkman and Goldman, now age twenty-three,
conspired in a plot to kill Henry Clay Frick, the manager of a steel
plant in Pennsylvania that had just witnessed a day-long fight between

Alexander Berkman (left) and Emma Goldman (right).

strikers and guards that left seven guards and nine strikers dead.

On July 23, 1892, Berkman walked into Frick's office, shot him three times and then stabbed him repeatedly. A group of workers responded to the fracas and beat Berkman into unconsciousness. Berkman was sentenced to over twenty years in prison, but investigators could not find enough evidence to charge Goldman.

On August 21, 1893, Emma Goldman delivered a speech to over three thousand mostly

Johann Most.

unemployed workers gathered in Union Square. During the speech, she encouraged the workers to "demand work. If they do not give you work, demand bread. If they deny you both, take bread."

Authorities considered the speech too radical and arrested Goldman a week later for "inciting a riot" (even though no riot actually occurred). Goldman was sentenced to one year in prison, where she began to study medicine after befriending a visiting doctor. Upon release from prison, Goldman studied medicine in Europe, earning two diplomas specializing in midwifery and massage. After graduation, she returned to the States to write and lecture and supported herself as a midwife and nurse.

In November 1899, she returned to Europe and met Hippolyte Havel; together they helped organize the International Anarchist Congress in Paris, France.

On September 6, 1901, President William McKinley was giving a speech in Buffalo, New York, when an unemployed factory worker named Leon Czolgosz emerged from the crowd and fired two bullets into McKinley's chest and abdomen. McKinley died eight days later, and authorities tied Emma Goldman to the assassination,

208 East Thirteenth
Street today.

The Emma Goldman
plaque.

claiming that Czolgosz was working on her behalf. Goldman was
arrested but was released two weeks later when authorities figured
out that there was no real link between the two.

In 1906, Emma Goldman began her own magazine, a radical
anarchist journal called *Mother Earth*, which she ran out of this
apartment. Alexander Berkman, released from prison the same
year, was the magazine's editor from 1907 to 1915.

In 1910, Goldman published the groundbreaking book *Anarchism
and Other Essays*.

In 1917, Goldman and Berkman were arrested when their newly
organized No Conscription League of New York offices were raided.

## East Houston Street to East Fourteenth Street:
## A Radical New Direcation

Goldman spent the next two years in prison and was deported to Russia upon her release.

### 310 East Thirteenth Street

On January 21, 1908, a bomb exploded on the first floor of this tenement building that tore up the staircase and shattered windows, sending residents fleeing in panic. This bombing was the result of yet another Black Hand threat and one of two such bombings on the same evening.

### 354 East Thirteenth Street

On May 21, 1921, five-year-old Giuseppe Varotta was kidnapped by a local Italian gang while playing in front of this building, his family's home. This gang dominated this blue-collar Italian enclave with hangouts at 410 and 430 East Thirteenth Street. There was a rumor in the neighborhood that the boy's father had won a $10,000 insurance settlement. This rumor made the family a target for the mob, which held Giuseppe for ransom. The problem was, the rumor was false, and the family could not afford the ransom. When police started snooping around, the gang murdered the boy. Authorities found his body floating in the Hudson River a week after the kidnapping.

A vigilante mob turned on the suspects and held them for the boy's father and neighbors, who beat them mercilessly. One of the gang members suffered brain damage, and all were sentenced to prison.

### 428 East Thirteenth Street

On April 26, 1895, Maria Barberi slit her lover Dominico Cataldi's throat in a saloon located here. She almost became the first woman put to death by the electric chair in the United States but escaped all charges with just a few days of psychiatric evaluation. Her alibi? He was cheating on her.

### 445 East Thirteenth Street

On January 6, 1908, a Black Hand threat led to the bombing of a saloon at this location, after owner Frank Locurio failed to answer an extortion note.

### 515 East Thirteenth Street

On the morning of August 28, 1895, thirty-four-year-old unemployed butcher Charles Tuskolka demanded money from his wife, Annie Tuskolka. When Annie refused, Charles retrieved a large butcher knife and began to hack Annie to death.

Annie owned a small restaurant at 114 East Fourth Street named the Little Waldorf and cared for five children, while Charles was recently unemployed and depended on Annie for money.

On this morning, after being refused money several times, Charles sent the children out to play and gave Annie one last chance. While sharpening a kitchen instrument, he told Annie to "give me money or die." Young Annie fought for her life but was eventually overcome and butchered. Charles then washed his hands, changed his clothing and went to a friend's bar at 162 East Fourth Street. At the bar, Charles ordered two glasses of seltzer and threw $100 on the bar as he left, stating, "Here, keep this to bury me with."

Charles was captured a short time later because his eldest daughter, sensing trouble, had not gone out to play with the other children. She witnessed the terrible murder by peeking through the keyhole. As a result, she reported the incident to neighbors and police.

# East Fourteenth Street

### 62 East Fourteenth Street

By 1920, former gang leader Monk Eastman was trying to lead a life along the straight and narrow. He was now a decorated war hero, after fighting for the U.S. Army in Europe during World War I, but he couldn't catch a break on the streets. So he got involved with a crooked Prohibition agent, who on December 26 of that year shot and killed Eastman in a drunken dispute on the sidewalk outside this address.

## 106 East Fourteenth Street

This corner was the site of Huber's Dime Museum in the late nineteenth century. The museum featured sideshow performers and magic shows. Harry Houdini was showcased here, as well as Dr. Henry S. Tanner, who survived a forty-day public fast at the museum in 1880. The Great Harry Houdini grew up in New York City after his family moved here from Wisconsin (by way of Hungary). A set of Houdini's handcuffs can be viewed at McSorley's Pub (15 East Seventh Street), New York City's oldest continuously run alehouse.

## 147 East Fourteenth Street

The parking lot just east of the Con Edison building is the site of what was the second location of the great political machine Tammany Hall.

Tammany Hall's first headquarters were located downtown near city hall; they moved into a building on this site in 1867. Tammany remained here until 1928, when it sold the building to Consolidated Gas and moved to its third and final location, at 100–102 East Seventeenth Street (the present-day New York Film Academy building), where it only lasted a couple of years before finally going out of business. Tammany Hall was a notoriously corrupt political organization with very close ties to the criminal underworld of the Lower East Side.

## 220 East Fourteenth Street

As early as 1921, "enthusiastic" supporters of Italian dictator Benito Mussolini were organizing in America. Many of the fascist sympathizers were made up of Italian veterans of World War I who had immigrated

Benito Mussolini.

to the United States after the war. One of the largest of these groups, the eight-hundred-member Fascio Centrale, was headquartered at this address. It had over thirty branches in Italian communities throughout the United States, including Chicago and Detroit.

Fascio Centrale was founded by Gelasio Caetani, with the blessing of Mussolini. In fact, Caetani was Mussolini's first ambassador to the United States. His mission was to harvest a good relationship with the United States, secure loans and work out trade agreements. He found that existing Mussolini supporters in the United States were basically bad for publicity, so he set up a unified organization with the intention of softening the dictator's image.

Caetani's plan did not work out the way he had hoped. Despite his pleas to American fascist groups to stay out of trouble and concentrate on charitable events, public opinion of the Italian government grew wearier. Incidents of violence and hysteria perpetuated by the media made Caetani's mission nearly impossible. Headlines like "Fascists Invade United States" made Mussolini question the idea of being connected to a foreign political organization on American soil, and he pulled his support for the project.

Caetani continued to operate Fascio Centrale, but without the support of the Italian government, radical members of the group split off and returned to the old way of violence and intimidation, vowing to fight "Socialist opponents on the streets." The "Black Shirts," as they were called, went on to initiate several attacks on innocent civilians over the next few years. One of the group's main enemies was newspaper publisher Carlo Tresca, an antifascist activist who ran the Italian-language newspaper *Il Martello* ("the Hammer") from 208 East Twelfth Street. Tresca was killed in 1944.

# BIBLIOGRAPHY

Anbinder, Tyler. *Five Points*. New York: Free Press, 2001.

Asbury, Herbert. *Gangs of New York*. New York: Thunder's Mouth Press, 2001.

Blum, Howard. *Gangland*. New York: Simon & Schuster, 1993.

Burbank, Jeff. *Las Vegas Babylon: True Tales of Glitter, Glamour and Greed*. New York: Franz Steiner Verlag, 2006.

Colladay, Morrison, and John J. O'Neill. *Nikola Tesla: Incredible Scientist*. [Kila], MT: Kessinger Pub. Co., n.d.

DeStefano, Anthony M. *King of the Godfathers*. New York: Kensington Pub., 2006.

Doesticks, Q.K. Philander. *The Witches of New York*. Upper Saddle River, NJ: Literature House, 1969.

English, T.J. *Paddy Whacked*. New York: Regan Books, 2005.

Feder, Sid, and Joachim Joesten. *The Luciano Story*. New York: D. McKay Co., 1954.

Feirstein, Sanna. *Naming New York: Manhattan Places & How They Got Their Names*. New York: NYU Press, 2001.

Fijnaut, Cyrille, and James B. Jacobs. *Organized Crime and Its Containment*. Boston: Kluwer Law and Taxation Publishers, 1991.

Fried, Albert. *The Rise and Fall of the Jewish Gangster in America*. New York: Holt, Rinehart and Winston, 1980.

Janvier, Thomas. *In Old New York: A Classic History of New York City*. New York: St. Martin's Press, 2000.

Kelly, William. *The 1929 Atlantic City Organized Crime Convention.* N.p., n.d.

Lardner, James. *NYPD: A City and Its Police.* New York: Henry Holt & Co., 2000.

Lavigne, Yves. *Hell's Angels: Three Can Keep a Secret if Two Are Dead.* N.p.: Lyle Stuart, 1989.

Maeder, Jay. *Big Town, Big Time: A New York Epic : 1898–1998.* New York: Daily News, 1999.

McCarty, John. *Bullets over Hollywood.* Cambridge, MA: Da Capo Press, 2005.

McIllwain, Jeffrey Scott. *Organizing Crime in Chinatown.* Jefferson, NC: McFarland & Co., 2004.

Mele, Christopher. *Selling the Lower East Side.* Minneapolis: University of Minnesota Press, 2000.

Miller, Nathan. *New World Coming.* New York: Scribner, 2003.

Morgan, Bill. *The Beat Generation in New York: A Walking Tour of Jack Kerouac's City.* San Francisco: City Lights Books, 1997

Moss, Frank. *The American Metropolis.* New York: P.F. Collier, 1897.

Mustain, Gene, and Jerry Capeci. *Mob Star: The Story of John Gotti.* Indianapolis: Alpha Books, 2002.

Nash, Jay Robert. *World Encyclopedia of Organized Crime.* New York: Paragon House, 1992.

Nelli, Humbert. *The Business of Crime: Italians and Syndicate Crime in the United States.* New York: Oxford University Press, 1976.

Newark, Tim. *Mafia Allies: The True Story of America's Secret Alliance with the Mob in World War II.* N.p.: MBI Publishing Company, 2007.

Raab, Selwyn. *Five Families.* New York: Thomas Dunne Books, 2005.

Ray, Pamela J., and James E. Files. *Interview with History: The J.F.K. Assassination.* Bloomington, IN: AuthorHouse, 2008.

Reppetto, Thomas A. *American Mafia.* New York: H. Holt, 2004.

————. *Bringing Down the Mob.* New York: H. Holt, 2006.

Riis, Jacob August. *How the Other Half Lives.* New York: Dover, 1971.

Russell, Dick. *The Man Who Knew Too Much.* New York: Carroll and Graf Publishers, 1992.

Sante, Luc. *Low Life*. New York: Farrar Strauss Giroux, 1991.

Scoville, Joseph Alfred. *The Old Merchants of New York City*. New York: Carleton, 1863–70.

Silverstone, Howard, CPA, and Michael Sheetz, JD. *Forensic Accounting and Fraud Investigation for Non-Experts*. Hoboken, NJ: Wiley, 2007.

Swartzman, Paul. *New York Notorious: A Borough-By-Borough Tour of the City's Most Infamous Crime Scenes*. New York: Crown Publishers, 1992.

United States Senate Committee on the Judiciary. *Hearing: Organized Crime in America*. Washington, D.C.: United States Government Printing Office, 1983.

Valentine, Douglas. *The Strength of the Wolf*. New York: Verso, 2004.

Valone, Thomas. *Harnessing the Wheelwork of Nature*. Kempton, IL: Adventure Unlimited Press, 2002.

Zito, Chuck, Joe Layden and Sean Penn. *Street Justice*. N.p.: Macmillan, 2003.

# Additional Sources

Department of Buildings Records
Encyclopedias
Local historians, friends and family
Municipal Archives Newspaper Archives
New York City Obituary Records
New York City Police Records
New York Public Library

Please visit us at
www.historypress.net